Ancient
Church Orders

Paul F. Bradshaw

Emeritus Professor of Liturgy
University of Notre Dame, USA

Contents

	Abbreviations	3
	Introduction	4
1	The Texts and Their Relationship	10
2	Living Literature	27
3	Layers of Tradition	43

The cover picture is from the German bible printed by Frisner and Sensenschmidt at Nuremberg, about 1476.
ISSN: 0951-2667
ISBN: 978-1-84825-780-1

Printed by Hobbs the Printers Ltd, Brunel Road, Totton, Hampshire SO40 3WX.

Abbreviations

A/GJLS	Alcuin/GROW Joint Liturgical Study
CSCO	Corpus Scriptorum Christianorum Orientalium
EO	*Ecclesia Orans*
JECS	*Journal of Early Christian Studies*
JTS	*Journal of Theological Studies*
PG	*Patrologia Graeca*, ed. J.-P. Migne
PO	*Patrologia Orientalis*
RevSR	*Revue des sciences religieuses*
SC	*Sources chrétiennes*
TU	Texte und Untersuchungen

Acknowledgements

I wish to record my indebtedness to the Institute of Sacred Music at Yale Divinity School for electing me as a Visiting Fellow for the fall semester 2014, which gave me the time and access to library resources to do the research for this book.

Introduction

Among the extant literature from the first few Christian centuries are a number of manuscripts that have come to be known collectively as church orders and purport to offer authoritative 'apostolic' prescriptions on Christian life and ecclesiastical practice. Prior to 1800, only one such work was generally known, the *Apostolic Constitutions*, first published in full in 1563 by Francisco Torres. During the nineteenth century, however, discoveries of others came thick and fast. In 1843, J. W. Bickell published the Greek text of a short treatise which he called the *Apostolic Church Order*.[1] In 1848 Henry Tattam produced an edition of what turned out to be a translation into the Bohairic dialect of Coptic, made as recently as 1804, of a composite work comprising three elements: (1) Bickell's *Apostolic Church Order*; (2) another previously unknown document, which, for want of a better title, was later designated as the 'Egyptian Church Order' until it was (mis-)identified as the *Apostolic Tradition* of *Hippolytus* in the early twentieth century; and (3) a different recension of the final Book 8 of the *Apostolic Constitutions*.[2] This collection is usually called the *Alexandrine Sinodos* or the *Clementine Heptateuch* (because it is divided into seven books and because Clement of Rome was in ancient times believed to have been the intermediary of apostolic teaching).

In 1854, Paul de Lagarde edited a Syriac version of a document generally referred to as the *Didascalia Apostolorum*;[3] and in 1856, he published a Syriac translation of the *Apostolic Church Order* and the Greek text of a work known as the *Epitome of Apostolic Constitutions* 8.[4] In 1870, Daniel von Haneberg produced the Arabic text of what claimed to be the

---
[1] J. W. Bickell, *Geschichte des Kirchenrechts* I (Meyer, Giessen, 1843), pp. 107–32.
[2] Henry Tattam, *The Apostolical Constitutions or the Canons of the Apostles in Coptic with an English Translation* (Oriental Translation Fund, London, 1848).
[3] Paul de Lagarde, *Didascalia Apostolorum syriace* (Teubner, Leipzig, 1854 = Zeller, Osnabrück, 1967 = Gorgias Press, Piscataway, NJ, 2010).
[4] Paul de Lagarde, *Reliquiae iuris ecclesiastici antiquissimae* (Teubner, Leipzig, 1856 = Zeller, Osnabrück, 1967), pp. 1–23.

Canons of Hippolytus;[5] and in 1875, Philotheos Bryennios discovered the only known Greek manuscript of the *Didache*, or 'Teaching of the Twelve Apostles', which he published in 1883.[6] In the same year, Lagarde revealed the existence of a Sahidic dialect version of the Bohairic collection earlier published by Tattam,[7] and in 1899, Ignatius Rahmani produced a Syriac document, the *Testamentum Domini*, which feigned to be the words of Jesus himself to the apostles after his resurrection.[8] In 1900, Edmund Hauler edited a fifth-century palimpsest from Verona which contained Latin translations of the *Didascalia*, the *Apostolic Church Order* and the 'Egyptian Church Order'.[9] Finally, in 1904, George Horner contributed Arabic and Ethiopic versions of the *Alexandrine Sinodos* to the Bohairic and Sahidic texts earlier published by Tattam and Lagarde.[10]

Although when first discovered some of these were accepted as authentic products of the apostolic age, by the beginning of the twentieth century their spurious character was generally recognized. However, while what these pseudo-apostolic texts have to say about the apostolic age itself may no longer be of interest, they remain potentially valuable sources of information for the thought and practices of the particular historical periods in which they actually emerged, and, as will become clear in the course of this study, for the subsequent centuries during which they were transmitted and often translated into other languages. Indeed, although they were all apparently originally written in Greek, in some cases all that has survived are these translations.

Although these works have generally been given the collective

---

[5] Daniel von Haneberg, *Canones S. Hippolyti arabice* (Munich, 1870 = Kessinger, Whitefish, MT, 2010).
[6] Philotheos Bryennios, *DIDACHE TON DODEKA APOSTOLON* (Voutyra, Constantinople, 1883).
[7] Paul de Lagarde, *Aegyptiaca* (Hoyer, Göttingen, 1883 = Zeller, Osnabrück, 1972), pp. 209–91.
[8] Ignatius Rahmani, *Testamentum Domini nostri Jesu Christi* (Kirchheim, Mainz, 1899 = Olms, Hildesheim, 1968).
[9] Edmund Hauler, *Didascaliae apostolorum fragmenta Veronensia latina. Accedunt canonum qui dicuntur apostolorum et aegyptiorum reliquiae* (Teubner, Leipzig, 1900).
[10] George Horner, *The Statutes of the Apostles or Canones Ecclesiastici* (Williams & Norgate, London, 1904).

designation of 'church orders', occasional voices have been raised against the use of this term for some or all of them, chiefly on the grounds of the disparities of form and contents that exist between the individual members of the group.[11] It is certainly the case that shared characteristics between the various church orders can only be said to be present with some considerable qualification. They are quite unlike the sixteenth-century Reformation texts which had been given this same designation, not least because the latter were understood to derive their authority from the particular ecclesiastical community that produced them and so could be subsequently changed by that same community, whereas the ancient church orders all claimed to derive their authority from being in some way 'apostolic'.

Yet, even the meaning of that term appears to differ from document to document as the literature evolved. Thus, beyond the title, 'The teaching of the twelve apostles' (which may or may not belong to the oldest form of the text), the *Didache* makes no other claims concerning the source of its material; and the *Apostolic Tradition* and *Canons of Hippolytus*, while asserting that what they are teaching is in accordance with the apostolic tradition that has come down to them, do not suggest that it derives verbatim from the mouths of the original apostles. Not so, however, the *Didascalia*, which inserts just before the last chapter of the work an alleged account of the composition of the document by a council of the twelve. The compilers of the *Apostolic Church Order* and of the *Apostolic Constitutions* go further and distribute their contents between the apostles, putting a different injunction into the mouth of each one, and the *Testamentum Domini* caps the whole process by attributing the teaching not just to the apostles but to Jesus himself. Thus only some of the church orders resemble works like the Pastoral Epistles or other early Christian apocryphal writings in being actually pseudepigraphical.

---

[11] On the history of the designation of these works as 'church orders', see Nancy Pardee, *The Genre and Development of the Didache*, Wissenschaftliche Untersuchungen zum Neuen Testament 2. Reihe 339 (Mohr Siebeck, Tübingen, 2012), pp. 31-46.

Although they are quite diverse in their literary character, what they do have in common is that they offer detailed prescriptions on matters of moral conduct, ecclesiastical organization and discipline, and liturgical practice. Yet, once again, the balance between these various elements differs from one work to another. As we shall see later, the *Didache* and the *Apostolic Church Order* combine a source containing *paraenesis* on the Christian life as a whole – catechesis on the moral conduct of the members of the church – with what might be called church order material proper. In the case of the *Apostolic Church Order*, this comprises directions about the appointment of ministers and their duties, and in the case of the *Didache* the conduct of other ecclesiastical practices as well. The *Didascalia* mixes both kinds of material together, but with the *Apostolic Tradition* and the other church orders we encounter literature of a very different kind. Here, at least in their extant form, exhortations concerning Christian behaviour and the qualities required of ordained ministers have largely disappeared, and are replaced by directives about the correct procedure to be adopted in the appointment of ministers, the texts of prayers to be used for ordination and in the celebration of the Eucharist, the ritual to be followed in the administration of baptism and other such matters. It is the ordering of the church and its liturgy which is now the principal focus.

Joseph Mueller in particular has challenged the idea that they constitute a single literary genre of their own because the forms and topics that have been identified as characteristic of them can also be found in what are clearly other genres. Instead, he claimed that they formed part of a wider exegetical tradition that extracted doctrine on church life from the Old Testament.[12] Building on the work of C. E. Fonrobert, who saw the *Didascalia* as a sort of Christian Mishnah, and of Eva Synek, who viewed the *Apostolic Constitutions* as a Christian Talmud,[13] he argued

---

[12] Joseph G. Mueller, 'The Ancient Church Order Literature: Genre or Tradition?' in *JECS* 15 (2007), pp. 337–80.
[13] Charlotte Elisheva Fonrobert, 'The *Didascalia Apostolorum*: A Mishnah for the Disciples of Jesus' in *JECS* 9 (2001), pp. 483–509; Eva M. Synek, 'Die Apostolischen Konstitutionen – ein "christlicher Talmud" aus dem 4. Jh.' in *Biblica* 79 (1998), pp. 27–56.

that the compilers of the various church orders intended their works to function as teaching on community order founded on interpretations of Old Testament material that adopted hermeneutical techniques used by Jews in the first centuries of the time, a mix of *halakah* and *haggadah*. But this, he asserted, was also true of a much broader tradition within early Christian writings, among them I Clement, Ambrose of Milan's *De sacramentis*, and the *Epistula apostolorum*.

However, although individual points of congruity may be seen between that tradition and some parts of some of the church orders, it will hardly suffice as a category for them all. For example, to describe them as being 'exegesis of Scripture' misrepresents them. When the Old Testament is cited, it is in support of the teaching that is given: the teaching is not derived from it. And unlike the Mishnah, alternative opinions of authorities are not offered.[14] Nevertheless, in spite of the difficulties associated with assigning a common classification to the church orders and the application of that term itself to them, they can be said to belong together partly because a literary relationship exists between many of them and also because in antiquity they were seen to have some affinity with one another and were accordingly assembled in collective works.

The first part of this present study to a large extent updates and corrects the chapter on church orders in my *Search for the Origins of Christian Worship* (2nd edn, SPCK, London/ Oxford University Press, New York, 2002) before going on to consider the impact of the latest scholarship on the way that the contents of these varied works should now be understood and used in the task of reconstructing the life and worship of early Christianity. Those readers who wish to have a more detailed account of the individual church orders than is given here

---

[14] For a more detailed critique, see Pardee, *The Genre and Development of the Didache*, pp. 18–31; also the comments by Alistair Stewart-Sykes, *The Didascalia Apostolorum: An English version with Introduction and Annotation* (Brepols, Turnhout, 2009), p. 4, n. 3.

and a guide to a more extensive bibliography of editions, translations, and secondary literature relating to them are referred to the works by Bruno Steimer, *Vertex Traditionis: Die Gattung der altchristlichen Kirchenordnungen* (De Gruyter, Berlin/New York, 1992) and by Johannis Mühlsteiger, *Kirchenordnungen: Anfänge kirchlicher Rechtsbildung* (Duncker & Humblot, Berlin, 2006).

1

The Texts and Their Relationship

As the various church orders began to appear in the latter half of the nineteenth century, it soon became obvious that they were more than merely parallel examples of a particular type of literature. Several of them exhibited such a marked similarity to one another that it clearly pointed to a direct literary relationship. There was no shortage of theories as to how they were connected, and almost every possible combination was suggested. Thus in 1891, Hans Achelis proposed that the genealogy ran from the *Canons of Hippolytus* through the so called 'Egyptian Church Order', and also another work that he thought had subsequently been lost, to the *Epitome* and then to *Apostolic Constitutions*[1] while in the same year F. X. Funk suggested almost exactly the opposite order: *Apostolic Constitutions* 8 → *Epitome* → 'Egyptian Church Order' → *Canons of Hippolytus*.[2] When Rahmani published the *Testamentum Domini* in 1899, he claimed that it was a second century work from which *Apostolic Constitutions* 8 and the 'Egyptian Church Order' were both derived,[3] with the *Canons of Hippolytus* in turn being dependent upon the latter. In 1901, John Wordsworth propounded the theory that there was a lost church order from which all these known ones had emanated.[4]

What is ironical to later eyes is that at this stage nobody proposed a

---

[1] Hans Achelis, *Die ältesten Quellen des orientalischen Kirchenrechtes. Erstes Buch: Die Canones Hippolyti*, TU 6/4 (Hinrichs, Leipzig, 1891).
[2] F. X. Funk, *Die apostolischen Konstitutionen, eine litterar historische Untersuchung* (Bader, Rottenburg, 1891 = Minerva, Frankfurt, 1970).
[3] Rahmani, *Testamentum Domini nostri Jesu Christi*.
[4] John Wordsworth, *The Ministry of Grace* (Longmans, Green & Co., London, 1901), pp. 18–21. A similar view was taken by A. J. Maclean, *The Ancient Church Orders* (Cambridge University Press, Cambridge, 1910 = Gorgias Press, Piscataway, New Jersey, 2004), pp. 141–73.

combination which would have put the 'Egyptian Church Order' first in this line. Instead, it was unanimously judged to be descended from one or other of the documents to which it had close similarity. It was not until the early twentieth century when it was (mis-)identified as the lost *Apostolic Tradition of Hippolytus* that it was taken seriously as being the original source of the other church orders from which it was formerly presumed to be derived. Even though modern scholarship would now challenge that attribution, the work remains universally recognized as the foundation document in that series. Thus, as can be seen from *Figure 1*, a family tree can now be established for the whole group of church orders with a high degree of certitude. Because they claim to be apostolic, they reveal neither the names of their true authors nor the place and date of their real origin, and hence such questions have been answered largely on the basis of the internal evidence of the works themselves.

Figure 1: The literary relationship between the church orders

(Two Ways material: see Chapter 2, *Figure 3* on page 30)

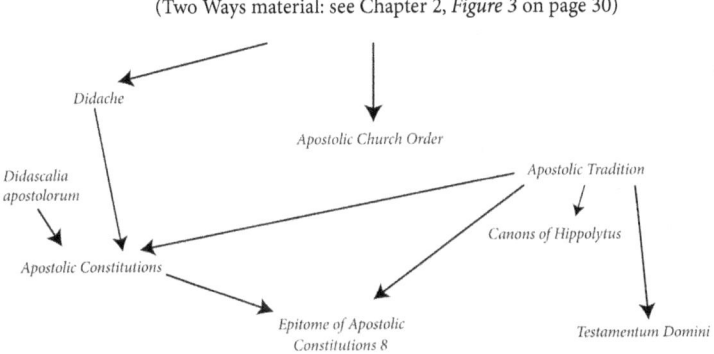

No new church orders have been added to the list of discoveries since the beginning of the twentieth century, but some new manuscripts of various recensions have been found, including in some cases a few small fragments of otherwise missing Greek originals. These have affected the task of establishing the text, and consequently better editions have since been produced for most of the individual documents, as will be noted in each case below.

The core texts

1. The *Didache*

The first part (chapters 1–6) is usually known as the 'Two Ways', because it presents moral teaching in the form of the way of life and the way of death. Then follow brief instructions about baptism (7), the practices of twice-weekly fasting (on Wednesdays and Fridays) and thrice-daily prayer (8), forms of prayer for use at a community meal (9–10), the treatment of 'apostles and prophets' (11–13), the celebration of the Eucharist 'on the Lord's Day of the Lord' (14),[5] and the appointment of bishops and deacons (15). It concludes with an admonition to eschatological vigilance (16).

At first, the only witness to the original was the Greek text discovered by Bryennios, but subsequently other Greek fragments were discovered at Oxyrhynchus and also parts of translations into Ethiopic and Coptic (although whether the latter is translated directly from the Greek or from Syriac has been disputed). A complete translation into Georgian has also been found, but scholars are divided over its antiquity: while the manuscript itself dates only from the nineteenth century, some think the translation may have been made in the fifth century.[6] It is also possible that there were once translations into Syriac and Latin, but these no longer exist.[7]

---

[5] Alistair Stewart(-Sykes), '*Didache* 14: Eucharistic?', in *Questions liturgiques* 93 (2012), pp. 3–16, claims that this chapter is not referring to the eucharist, but his argument rests on a rather questionable distinction between eucharistic and non-eucharistic community meals in early Christianity.

[6] Text in Willy Rordorf and André Tuilier, *La doctrine des douze apôtres*, SC 248 (Cerf, Paris, 1978); 2nd edn, SC 248bis (Cerf, Paris, 1998); English translation with commentary by Kurt Niederwimmer, *The Didache: A Commentary*, Hermeneia series (Fortress, Minneapolis, 1998).

[7] See Niederwimmer, *The Didache*, pp. 9, 12–13.

Most scholars have accepted the work as having originated in Syria (though Egypt has occasionally been suggested), but estimates of its date have varied widely. Some have placed it in the early second century, others assign it to the late first century, and some argue that it antedates many of the New Testament writings. Obviously, the literary dependence on other early Christian writings could be a significant point in establishing its date, but once again there has not been any scholarly consensus as to which, if any, of the New Testament books may have been known to the author.[8]

2. The *Apostolic Church Order*

After a short introduction (chapters 1–3), the first part of this small treatise (4–14) comprises 'Two Ways' material, and the second part (15–30) issues brief regulations for the appointment of bishops, presbyters, readers, deacons and widows, and directives concerning the duties of deacons, laymen and laywomen. It was given the name *Apostolic Church Order* when it was first published in 1843 by J. W. Bickell, although the title which appears in the Greek text is 'The instructions through Clement and canons of the holy Apostles', and it has also received

---

[8] Comprehensive bibliography of secondary literature in Aaron Milavec, *The Didache: Faith, Hope, and Life of the Earliest Christian Communities, 50–70 C.E.* (Newman Press, New York, 2003), pp. 916–53. More recent studies include: Alan Garrow, *The Gospel of Matthew's Dependence on the Didache* (T & T Clark, London/New York, 2004); Marcello del Verme, *Didache and Judaism: Jewish Roots of an Ancient Christian-Jewish Work* (T & T Clark, London/New York, 2004); Huub van de Sandt (ed.), *Matthew and the Didache* (Van Gorcum, Assen/Fortress, Minneapolis, 2005); Huub van de Sandt and Jurgen Zangenberg (eds), *Matthew, James, and the Didache: Three Related Documents in Their Jewish and Christian Settings* (Society of Biblical Literature, Atlanta, 2008); and several essays by Jonathan A. Draper, 'First-Fruits and the Support of Prophets, Teachers, and the Poor in Didache 13 in Relation to New Testament Parallels' in Andrew F. Gregory and Christopher M. Tuckett (eds), *Trajectories through the New Testament and the Apostolic Fathers* (Oxford University Press, Oxford/New York, 2005), pp. 223–43; 'The Holy Vine of David Made Known to the Gentiles through God's Servant Jesus: "Christian Judaism" in the Didache' in Matt Jackson-MacCabe (ed.), *Jewish Christianity Reconsidered* (Fortress, Minneapolis, 2007), pp. 257–83; 'Pure Sacrifice in Didache 14 as Jewish Christian Exegesis' in *Neotestamentica* 42 (2008), pp. 223–52; Thomas O'Loughlin, *The Didache: A Window on the earliest Christians* (SPCK, London, and Baker, Grand Rapids, MI, 2010).

other appellations, among them 'The Ecclesiastical Constitutions of the Apostles'. Only one manuscript, of the twelfth century, contains the entire Greek text; another, of the tenth century, contains an abbreviated form of it; a version of the *Two Ways* material found in chapters 4–14 is extant in three other codices, describing itself as 'The Epitome of the canons of the holy apostles'; and there are also Latin, Syriac, Sahidic, Bohairic, Arabic, and Ethiopic translations of the whole. It has been thought to have been written in Egypt, although some scholars have assigned it to Syria, and in its final form to date from the fourth century, but these conclusions too have recently been challenged by Alistair Stewart-Sykes and will be considered in the next chapter.[9]

3. The *Didascalia Apostolorum*

This very lengthy church order begins with admonitions concerning the Christian life (chapters 1–3), and continues with a substantial section on the qualifications, conduct, and duties of a bishop (4–11). The physical disposition of bishop, presbyters, deacons, lay men, lay women, and children in the church building is dealt with next (12), and the people are exhorted to be constant in their attendance at church, and to avoid heretical assemblies and pagan festivities (13). Then follow injunctions concerning widows (14–15), male and female deacons (16), and the adoption of orphans (17). Bishops and deacons are forbidden to accept alms from those leading evil lives or following unacceptable occupations (18), and all Christians are exhorted to care for those who are imprisoned for the faith, and to be ready to face persecution and death themselves, comforted by the hope of the resurrection (19–20). Every Wednesday and Friday in the year, and the six days prior to Easter, are to be observed as days of fasting (21), and the treatise then moves on to refer to the upbringing of children (22), and to denounce heresy and schism (23).

---

[9] Text, English translation and bibliography of secondary literature in Alistair Stewart-Sykes, *The Apostolic Church Order: The Greek Text with Introduction, Translation and Annotation*, Early Christian Studies 10 (St Pauls Publications, Strathfield, Australia, 2006).

Chapters 24 and 25 purport to describe the composition of the work by the apostles as a defence against heresy, and the final lengthy chapter (26) argues strongly for the freedom of Christians from the ritual legislation of the Old Testament.

With the exception of a small fragment of Chapter 15 and a reworked form of the document in *Apostolic Constitutions* 1–6, the original Greek has been lost, and knowledge of the text mainly rests on two early translations, one into Latin and the other into Syriac. The Latin is known only from the Verona palimpsest, which preserves about two fifths of the work. The Syriac, which thus constitutes the sole witness to the complete text, is preserved wholly or partially in a number of manuscripts, the oldest of which dates from the eighth century. The fourth century has been proposed as a possible date for this translation, but certain features of it might suggest a somewhat later period.[10] A possible Coptic fragment of the text has also been found,[11] but Arabic and Ethiopic versions are dependent on *Apostolic Constitutions* 1–6.

The *Didascalia* almost certainly originates in Syria, and the traditional consensus was that it was the work of a single author, with the possibility of only minor interpolations by others, composed during the first half of the third century, probably c. 230. From the prominence that it gave to the episcopate, it was concluded that its author might have been a bishop, and because he exhibited some medical knowledge, some supposed that he might also have been a physician. This consensus view has now been challenged by Alistair Stewart-Sykes, whose contribution will be considered in the next chapter.

---

[10] Syriac text in Arthur Vööbus, *The Didascalia Apostolorum in Syriac*, CSCO 401, 402, 407, 408; Scriptores Syri 175, 176, 179, 180 (Louvain 1979); English translation and substantial bibliography of secondary literature in Stewart-Sykes, *The Didascalia Apostolorum*.

[11] Alberto Camplani, 'A Coptic Fragment from the *Didascalia Apostolorum* (M579 f.1)' in *Augustinianum* 36 (1996), pp. 47–51.

4. The so-called *Apostolic Tradition of Hippolytus*

After a very brief prologue this church order begins with directions for the ordinations of a bishop, presbyter, and deacon, and provides an ordination prayer for each one. In the case of the episcopal ordination, it also sets out a specimen form of eucharistic prayer for the new bishop to use, although permitting him to substitute his own words if he wishes. It then proceeds to the appointment of widows, readers, virgins, subdeacons and those with the gift of healing. Lengthy instructions follow concerning the process of Christian initiation, beginning with the procedure for admission to the catechumenate and a list of occupations forbidden to prospective Christians, and continuing with the baptismal rite itself, which is intended for both adults and children and leads into the first communion of the neophytes. The final part of the work deals with other liturgical matters, among them the conduct of a community supper, the observance of a two-day fast before Easter, the times of daily prayer and instruction in the word, and the use of the sign of the cross.

Although traditionally identified as being the *Apostolic Tradition* by Hippolytus, in reality this is an anonymous and untitled text, and when first discovered was given the name 'The Egyptian Church Order'. In 1906, however, Eduard von der Goltz suggested that it might be this work by Hippolytus of Rome that had previously been thought had been lost.[12] His theory was taken up and elaborated, first by Eduard Schwartz in 1910, and then quite independently and much more fully by R. H. Connolly in 1916.[13] Thereafter, with a few exceptions, scholars accepted their conclusions and consequently dated its composition as having been in the early third century, until doubts were expressed about its

---

[12] Eduard von der Golz, 'Unbekannte Fragmente altchristlicher Gemeindeordnungen' in *Sitzungsberichte der Preussischen Akademie der Wissenschaften* (1906), pp. 141–57; see also idem, 'Die Taufgebete Hippolyts und andere Taufgebete der alten Kirchen' in *Zeitschrift für Kirchengeschichte* 27 (1906), pp. 1–51.

[13] Eduard Schwartz, *Über die pseudoapostolischen Kirchenordnungen* (Trübner, Strasbourg, 1910); R. H. Connolly, *The So-called Egyptian Church Order and Derived Documents* (Cambridge University Press, Cambridge, 1916 = Kraus, Nendeln, Liechtenstein, 1967).

attribution and date by several scholars in the late twentieth century, which has led to a substantial reconsideration of its character and provenance (about which much more will be said in the next chapter). Apart from a few Greek fragments, it survives only in translations into Latin, Sahidic, Bohairic, Arabic and Ethiopic.[14] A different version of the Ethiopic, in all probability derived directly from Greek and known to the translator of the other Ethiopic version, has recently been published by Alessandro Bausi, which may offer new insights for the reconstruction of its Greek original.[15]

Derivative texts

The *Apostolic Tradition* was subsequently re-worked in two other church orders and, along with other works, formed part of a third.

1. The *Canons of Hippolytus*

Although attention had been drawn as early as the seventeenth century to this Arabic collection of 38 canons with a concluding sermon, Haneberg's 1870 edition was the first published text, and it was from this that Achelis made his 1891 translation into Latin, containing many doubtful conjectures. As indicated at the beginning of this chapter, Achelis accepted the attribution to Hippolytus as genuine and arrived at the conclusion that this was the original from which all the other church orders containing similar material were derived. As a consequence, interest was aroused in the document among liturgical scholars, but,

---

[14] English translation, commentary and bibliography of secondary literature in Paul F. Bradshaw, Maxwell E. Johnson and L. Edward Phillips, *The Apostolic Tradition: A Commentary*, Hermeneia series (Fortress, Minneapolis, 2002), and, from a rather more conservative position, in Alistair Stewart-Sykes, *Hippolytus: On the Apostolic Tradition* (St Vladimir's Seminary Press, Crestwood, NY, 2001).

[15] Text and Italian translation in Alessandro Bausi, 'La nuova versione Etiopica della Traditio Apostolica: edizione e traduzione preliminare' in Paola Buzi and Alberto Camplani (eds), *Christianity in Egypt: Literary Production and Intellectual Trends*, Studia Ephemeridis Augustinianum 125 (Institutum patristicum Augustinianum, Rome, 2011), pp. 19–69.

after the researches of Schwartz and Connolly had demonstrated that it was in reality merely a derivative of the *Apostolic Tradition*, it came to be considered as the latest of the group of related church orders, dating from the fifth or sixth century, and interest in it declined.

However, in 1956, Bernard Botte suggested that it had been composed in Egypt around the middle of the fourth century,[16] and in 1966, René Georges Coquin, in the first and only proper critical edition of the text, followed up and amplified Botte's arguments, proposing on the basis of internal evidence a date between 336 and 340 for the work.[17] Christoph Markschies, however, has subsequently argued that, while the lost Greek original may date from that period, both the text in the form in which we now have it and the attribution to Hippolytus are no older than the late fourth or early fifth century.[18] Nevertheless, as the earliest known derivative of the *Apostolic Tradition*, some of what have been thought to be drastic recastings of that work may possibly be points at which it alone has retained primitive readings that have been revised by the other later witnesses to the text.

Although it is now extant only in Arabic, there is general agreement that it is derived from a lost Coptic version, which was in turn a translation of an original Greek text. Coquin considered that it had been written by a priest rather than a bishop – though his arguments are not totally convincing – and that its place of composition was Alexandria: this latter view was later challenged by Heinzgerd Brakmann, who argued that it originated from elsewhere in northern Egypt.[19]

---

[16] Bernard Botte, 'L'origine des Canons d'Hippolyte' in *Mélanges en l'honneur de Mgr Michel Andrieu* (Palais Universitaire, Strasbourg, 1956), pp. 53–63.

[17] René Georges Coquin, *Les Canons d'Hippolyte*, PO 31/2 (Firmin-Didot, Paris, 1966); English translation based on this edition in Paul F. Bradshaw, *The Canons of Hippolytus*, A/GJLS 2 (Grove Books, Nottingham, 1987).

[18] Christoph Markschies, 'Wer schrieb die sogenannte *Traditio Apostolica*? Neue Beobachtungen und Hypothesen zu einer kaum lösbaren Frage aus der altkirchen Literaturgeschichte' in Wolfram Kinzig, Christoph Markschies and Markus Vinzent, *Tauffragen und Bekenntnis*, Arbeiten zur Kirchengeschichte 74 (De Gruyter, Berlin/New York, 1999), pp. 8–43, here at pp. 8–11, 63–69.

[19] Heinzgerd Brakmann ,'Alexandreia und die Kanones des Hippolyt' in *Jahrbuch für Antike und Christentum* 22 (1979), pp. 139–49.

2. The *Testamentum Domini*

This church order is a much enlarged version of the *Apostolic Tradition*, set within the context of instructions given by Jesus himself to his disciples before his ascension, and beginning with an apocalyptic discourse. The author displays a somewhat perverse fidelity to his principal source: although he has retained most of its wording, he has interpolated so much material of his own that it frequently has an entirely different appearance and sense from the original. Thus all the various prayers are retained, but in a much expanded form, and others are added.

The original Greek text is lost,[20] and reliance has usually been placed on the Syriac version published by Rahmani,[21] but here there are two problems. First, his edition was based on only one family of manuscripts, while a different manuscript tradition seems to underlie the text of the *Testamentum Domini* found in the *West Syrian Synodicon*,[22] which may offer indications of better readings at some points. Second, even if the earliest text of the Syriac can be established, it is not certain that it always accurately reproduced the original Greek, especially as there are also extant Arabic and Ethiopic versions of the document with significantly different readings. Although these have been thought to be dependent upon a lost Coptic translation, René Georges Coquin believed that at least some of the Ethiopic translations had been made directly from

---

[20] Although a fragment remains: see Simon Corcoran and Benet Salway, 'The Newly Identified Greek Fragment of the *Testamentum Domini*' in *JTS* 62 (2011), pp. 118–35. A Georgian version also appears to have existed at one time: see Tinatin Chronz and Heinzgerd Brakmann, 'Fragmente des Testamentum Domini in georgischer Übersetzung' in *Zeitschrift für Antikes Christentum* 13 (2009) 395–402.

[21] English translation by James Cooper and A. J. Maclean, *The Testament of Our Lord Translated into English from the Syriac* (T & T Clark, Edinburgh, 1902); partial English translation and bibliography of secondary literature in Grant Sperry-White, *The Testamentum Domini: A Text for Students*, A/GJLS 19 (Grove Books, Nottingham, 1991).

[22] Text and English translation in Arthur Vööbus (ed.), *The Synodicon in the West Syrian Tradition*, CSCO 367, 368; Scriptores Syri 161, 162 (Louvain 1975–1976). This is based on MS. 8/11 of the Syrian Orthodox Patriarchate of Damascus, 1204 C.E.

the Greek.²³ At first any comparison with these versions was extremely problematic, as neither had ever been published, but in 1984 Robert Beylot produced a critical edition of the Ethiopic, which goes some way to meet the difficulty.²⁴ Since both these versions are later than the Syriac, many differences can be dismissed as the emendations – intentional and unintentional – of translators and copyists, but at least at some points they may retain older readings. The doxologies in the Ethiopic, for example, have a much simpler – and hence seemingly more primitive – form than those in the Syriac.²⁵

It has traditionally been believed that the work originated in Syria, though Asia Minor and Egypt have also been suggested, and dated from the fifth century. While Grant Sperry-White in 1991 proposed its origin as being earlier, around 381, Michael Kohlbacher has more recently argued for the second half of the fifth century and from a settlement of ascetics and charismatics on the coast of Gaza.²⁶

3. The *Apostolic Constitutions*

The *Didascalia*, *Didache* and *Apostolic Tradition* were collected, reworked and expanded along with other material²⁷ to form this composite

---

[23] René Georges Coquin, 'Le Testamentum Domini. Problèmes de tradition textuelle' in *Parole de l'Orient* 5 (1974), pp. 165–88.

[24] Robert Beylot, *Le Testamentum Domini éthiopien* (Peeters, Louvain, 1984). Its quality was, however, questioned in a review by Roger Cowley, *Journal of Semitic Studies* 31 (1986), pp. 292–5

[25] Compare the Syriac, 'to you be praise and to your only begotten Son our Lord Jesus Christ and to the Holy Spirit honourable and worshipped and life giving and consubstantial with you, now and before all worlds and to the generation of generations and to the ages of ages' (Rahmani, p. 99) with the Ethiopic, 'Glory to the Father, to the Son, and to the Holy Spirit, now and always and to the ages of ages' (Beylot, p. 206).

[26] Sperry-White, *The Testamentum Domini*, p. 6; Michael Kohlbacher, 'Wessen Kirche ordnete das Testamentum Domini Nostri Jesu Christi?', in Martin Tamcke and Andreas Heinz (eds), *Zu Geschichte, Theologie, Liturgie und Gegenwartslage der syirchen Kirchen* (LIT Verlag, Münster 2000), pp. 55–137.

[27] Including some prayers with a strongly Jewish flavour, about the nature of which there has been some debate: see David A. Fiensy, *Prayers Alleged to be Jewish: An Examination of the Constitutiones Apostolorum*, Brown Judaic Studies 65 (Scholars Press, Chico, California, 1985); Pieter W. van der Horst, 'The Greek Synagogue Prayers in the Apostolic Constitutions, Book VII' in Joseph Tabory

Greek church order, which is divided into eight books. It is generally accepted that it originated in Syria, and most probably in Antioch, between 375 and 380. It is unlikely to be much earlier than that, because it includes a reference to the feast of Christmas, which was only just beginning to make an appearance in eastern churches, and it is unlikely to be later, because its doctrine of the Holy Spirit is incompatible with the definition agreed at the Council of Constantinople in 381. The identity and theological position of the compiler, on the other hand, have been long debated. Indeed, the orthodoxy of the document became suspect at an early date, and it was thought by the Trullan Synod (691–2) that heretics must have falsified the original apostolic work. Photius, the patriarch of Constantinople (d. 891), criticized the whole compilation for its Arianism, although subsequently opinion was divided over this question.

Among modern scholars, Funk in his 1905 edition of the text (which has generally been treated as definitive) tended to play down the heterodoxy of the work by preferring orthodox variant readings wherever possible and by claiming that any suspect formulae came from the compiler's source and thus antedated the Arian controversy.[28] C. H. Turner criticized Funk's textual methods and argued strongly for an Arian compiler,[29] and Bernard Capelle later demonstrated that the text of the *Gloria in Excelsis* found in the *Apostolic Constitutions* was not the original form of the hymn, as had been thought, but that the

---

(ed.), *From Qumran to Cairo: Studies in the History of Prayer* (Hotsa'at Orhot, Jerusalem, 1999), pp. 32–6; Esther G. Chazon, 'A "Prayer Alleged to be Jewish" in the *Apostolic Constitutions*' in Esther G. Chazon et al. (eds), *Things Revealed: Studies in Early Jewish and Christian Literature in Honor of Michael E. Stone* (Brill, Leiden, 2004), pp. 261–77.

[28] F. X. Funk, *Didascalia et Constitutiones Apostolorum* (Schoeningh, Paderborn 1905 = Bottega d'Erasmo, Turin, 1979); English translation based on this edition in Alexander Roberts and James Donaldson (eds), *The Constitutions of the Holy Apostles*, Ante-Nicene Fathers 7 (Christian Literature Company, New York, 1886), pp. 387–505.

[29] C. H. Turner, 'A Primitive Edition of the Apostolic Constitutions and Canons' in *JTS* 15 (1913), pp. 53–65; idem, 'Notes on the Apostolic Constitutions' in *JTS* 16 (1914), pp. 54–61, 523–38; 21 (1920), pp. 160–8; 31 (1930), pp. 128–41.

compiler had changed a hymn addressed to Christ into one addressed to the Father.[30] Because of similarities of language with the longer recension of the letters of Ignatius of Antioch, scholars have usually concluded that the compiler, whatever his theological stance, was also the interpolator of these letters.

The most recent contributions to the authorship debate are by Georg Wagner (who drew linguistic parallels with the writings of Eunomius),[31] by Dieter Hagedorn (who attributed the composition to an obscure bishop named Julian),[32] and by Marcel Metzger, who built upon Hagedorn's suggestion and concluded that, although Julian's commentary on Job is much more explicitly Arian than the more moderate subordinationism of the *Apostolic Constitutions*, this difference could be explained by the fact that the latter was a liturgical work and so drew upon traditional material. Metzger did not think, however, that its compiler could be considered a strict Arian.[33] He also published a new edition of the text, making use of a wider range of manuscripts and free from the orthodox bias of Funk's edition.[34]

What is known as the *Epitome of Apostolic Constitutions* 8 is a series of five extracts from that book, each with its own subheading (1–2, 4–5, 16–28, 30–4, 42–6).[35] That for the second part is 'Constitutions

---

[30] Bernard Capelle, 'Le texte du "Gloria in excelsis"' in *Revue d'histoire ecclésiastique* 44 (1949), pp. 439–57.

[31] Georg Wagner, 'Zur Herfunkt der Apostolischen Konstitutionen' in *Mélanges liturgiques offerts au R. P. Dom Bernard Botte OSB* (Abbaye du Mont César, Louvain, 1972), pp. 525-37.

[32] Dieter Hagedorn, *Der Hiobkommentar des Arianers Julian* (De Gruyter, Berlin/New York, 1973), pp. XXXVII–LVII. See also T. A. Kopecek, 'Neo-Arian Religion: The Evidence of the Apostolic Constitutions' in R. C. Gregg (ed.), *Arianism: Historical and Theological Reassessments* (Patristic Foundation, Philadelphia, 1985 = Wipf & Stock, Eugene, OR, 2006), pp. 153–80..

[33] Marcel Metzger, 'La théologie des Constitutions apostoliques par Clément' in *RevSR* 57 (1983), pp. 29–49, 112–22, 169–94, 273–94.

[34] Marcel Metzger, *Les Constitutions apostoliques*, SC 320, 329, 336 (Cerf, Paris, 1985–7); partial English translation based on this edition in W. Jardine Grisbrooke, *The Liturgical Portions of the Apostolic Constitutions: A Text for Students*, A/GJLS 13–14 (Grove Books, Nottingham, 1990).

[35] Text in Funk, *Didascalia et Constitutiones Apostolorum* II, pp. 72–96. For further details, see Steimer, *Vertex Traditionis*, pp. 80–6.

of the Holy Apostles concerning ordinations through Hippolytus'. It has sometimes been thought to have been a preliminary draft of Book 8 but is more commonly held to be a later condensation of it, though incorporating some material directly from the *Apostolic Tradition* at two points – the prayer for the ordination of a bishop and the instructions for appointing a reader. In addition, one manuscript alone also has, for some reason or another, a similar version of *Apostolic Tradition* 23. Christoph Markschies, however, has contended that the compiler of the *Epitome* did not have access to the original Greek text of that church order as such, but to a version of it that had already undergone some modification.[36]

While usually limited to just the above listed texts, the category of church orders could be extended to encompass other works that made use of material from one or more of them as a source. These would include the Coptic *Canons of Basil*[37] and the Gallican *Statuta ecclesiae antiqua*.[38] Moreover, it might also be said to have progenitors in the household codes of the New Testament Epistles and in the directions about the qualities requisite for Christian ministers and the procedure for their appointment contained in the Pastoral Epistles.[39]

Collections

The majority of these church orders appear to have been gathered quite quickly into larger compilations of similar material. Indeed, most of the texts that are extant are known only through their presence in these collections and not as independent works. In addition to the assemblage

---

[36] Markschies, 'Wer schrieb die sogenannte *Traditio Apostolica*?', pp. 15–19.

[37] A sixth-century derivative of the *Canons of Hippolytus*; text in Wilhelm Riedel, *Die Kirchenrechtsquellen des Patriarchats Alexandrien* (Deichert, Leipzig, 1900 = Scientia Verlag, Aalen, 1968), pp. 231–83.

[38] Perhaps composed by Gennadius of Marseilles c. 490 and drawing upon both the *Apostolic Tradition* and the *Apostolic Constitutions*; text in Charles Munier, *Les Statuta ecclesiae antiqua* (Presses universitaires de France, Paris, 1960).

[39] See Steimer, *Vertex Traditionis*, pp. 159–90; Mühlsteiger, *Kirchenordnungen*, pp. 17–68.

in the *Apostolic Constitutions*, there are also three other somewhat similar collections:

- a Latin translation – unfortunately with many lacunae – of the *Didascalia*, the *Apostolic Church Order* and the *Apostolic Tradition*, thought to have been made about the same time as the *Apostolic Constitutions* but known to us only through one manuscript, the fifth-century Verona palimpsest;[40]
- what has been called the *Alexandrine Sinodos* or *Clementine Heptateuch*, found in several different linguistic versions – in the two dialects of Coptic (Sahidic and Bohairic), in Arabic and in Ethiopic (of which the Sahidic is the oldest and the others all in one way or another ultimately depend on it) – and comprising the *Apostolic Church Order*, the *Apostolic Tradition* and a different version of *Apostolic Constitutions* Book 8;[41]
- the *Clementine Octateuch*, which is found in different forms in two different languages, Syriac and Arabic, neither of which has yet ever been published in full,[42] and consists of the *Testamentum Domini*, followed by the material included in the *Alexandrine Sinodos*, except that the Syriac version differs from the Arabic in omitting the text of the *Apostolic Tradition* and consequently dividing the *Testamentum Domini* into two books in order to retain the eightfold form.

---

[40] First edited by Hauler, and most recently by Erik Tidner, *Didascaliae apostolorum, Canonum ecclesiasticorum, Traditionis apostolicae versiones Latinae*, TU 75 (Akademie-Verlag, Berlin, 1963).

[41] Sahidic in Lagarde, *Aegyptiaca*, pp. 209–91; Bohairic in Tattam, *The Apostolical Constitutions*; Arabic and Ethiopic in Horner, *The Statutes of the Apostles*; with a later edition of the Arabic and French translation by Jean and Augustin Périer, *Les 127 Canons des Apôtres*, PO 8/4 (Firmin-Didot, Paris, 1912 = Brepols, Turnhout, 1971).

[42] French translation of the Syriac in François Nau, *La version syriaque de l'octateuque de Clément* (Lethielleux, Paris 1913; re-edited by Pio Ciprotti: Lethielleux, Paris/Giuffre, Milan, 1967 = Gorgias Press, Piscataway, NJ, 2012); summary of the Arabic in Riedel, *Die Kirchenrechtsquellen des Patriarchats Alexandrien*, pp. 155–6. See also the announcement of the discovery of five new Syriac manuscripts by Arthur Vööbus, 'Nouvelles sources de l'octateuque clémentin syriaque' in *Le Muséon* 86 (1973), pp. 105–9. A critical edition with German translation is currently being prepared by a team led by Hubert Kaufhold.

Although the striking similarities in contents and order between these collections strongly suggest some literary relationship, the obvious one of direct dependency appears to be ruled out by the equally significant differences of language and structure that exist between them. Bernard Botte proposed that they were all ultimately derived from an early Greek 'tripartite collection', subsequently lost, which had consisted of the *Didascalia*, the *Apostolic Church Order*, and the *Apostolic Tradition* – in that order.[43] That suggestion, however, still left a number of questions unanswered, among them why both the *Sinodos* and the *Octateuch* should have chosen to add to this supposed triple collection a version of *Apostolic Constitutions* 8. Their history, therefore, appears to have been more complicated and closer to the theory put forward by J. M. Hanssens and later endorsed by Alexandre Faivre, that originally only the *Apostolic Church Order* and the *Apostolic Tradition* circulated together in the fourth century.[44] Hanssens argued that from this combination there developed two further collections: one comprising the *Didascalia*, the *Apostolic Church Order* and the *Apostolic Tradition*, from which the *Apostolic Constitutions* and the Latin translation were derived; the other made up of the *Apostolic Church Order*, the *Apostolic Tradition* and a version of *Apostolic Constitutions* 8. This latter document would thus have constituted the original Greek collection of which the *Alexandrine Sinodos* was a translation; and a conjectured Greek *Octateuch* would then have been an expanded form of this, prefixed by the *Testamentum Domini*. Yet, even this reconstruction of the text history leaves several questions of detail still unanswered, among them the origin of the Ethiopic version of the *Testamentum Domini* and also the existence of a

---

[43] Bernard Botte, 'Les plus anciennes collections canoniques' in *L'Orient syrien* 5 (1960), pp. 331–49.
[44] J. M. Hanssens, *La Liturgie d'Hippolyte: Ses documents, son titulaire, ses origines et son charactère*, Orientalia Christiana Analecta 155 (Pontificale Institutum Orientalium Studiorum, Rome, 1959, 2nd edn, 1965), pp. 171ff.; Alexandre Faivre, 'La documentation canonico-liturgique de l'église ancienne' in *RevSR* 54 (1980), pp. 204–15, 273–97 = Jean-Claude Fredouille and René-Michel Roberge (eds), *La documentation patristique: Bilan et prospective* (Presses de l'Université de Laval, Quebec/Presses de l'Université de Paris–Sorbonne, Paris, 1995), pp. 3–41, here at pp. 21, 24.

different version of the *Apostolic Tradition* in Ethiopic from that in the *Alexandrine Sinodos*.

Figure 2: The parallels between the collections

Apostolic Constitutions (Greek, divided into eight books)
Didascalia   Didache   Apostolic Tradition
(books 1–6)   (book 7)   (book 8)

Verona Palimpsest LV (53) (Latin)
Didascalia   Apostolic Church   Apostolic Tradition
                     Order

Alexandrine Sinodos/Clementine Heptateuch (Sahidic, Bohairic,[45] Arabic, Ethiopic)
                     Apostolic Church   Apostolic Tradition   Apostolic Constitutions 8
                     Order (book 1)   (books 2–3)   (books 4–7)

Clementine Octateuch (Arabic)
                     Testamentum   Apostolic Tradition   Apostolic Constitutions 8
                     Domini (book 1)   (books 2–3)   (books 4–7)

Clementine Octateuch (Syriac)
Testamentum   Apostolic Church   Apostolic Constitutions 8
Domini (books 1–2)   Order (book 3)   (books 4–8)

---

[45] The Bohairic version is sometimes described instead as being a translation of the *Clementine Octateuch* because, although it lacks the *Testamentum Domini* found in the Arabic and Syriac forms of that work, it is divided into eight books and not seven.

2

Living Literature

The *Didache* is usually treated as being the earliest of the church orders, but the material in the first half of the work, Chapters 1–6, evidently had an independent existence before being incorporated into this more extensive document. Forming a tractate on the two ways that a human being may go – the way of life and the way of death – it has not only antecedents and parallels in Jewish and other literature but more significantly a direct literary relationship with certain other early Christian writings.[1] These are:

- the *Epistle of Barnabas*, chapters 18–20, the work being variously dated between 95 and 125 CE;
- the *Doctrina apostolorum*, a Latin text existing in an incomplete manuscript that apparently dates from the ninth century and in a complete version from the eleventh century;
- the *Apostolic Church Order*, chapters 4–14, and its *Epitome*;
- part of the fifth-century Arabic *Life of Shenoute of Atripe*;
- sections of Pseudo-Athanasius, *Syntagma doctrinae* (PG 28.836–45) and the closely related material in *Fides patrum* (PG 28.1637–43).[2]

Earlier scholars expressed a variety of opinions as to the interrelationship of these several documents, but the conclusion reached by Kurt Niederwimmer after examining these theories was that Barnabas drew

---

[1] See Gérard-Henry Baudry, *La voie de la vie. Étude sur la catéchèse des Pères de l'Église*, Theologie historique 110 (Beauchesne, Paris, 1999); Alistair Stewart-Sykes, *On the Two Ways* (St Vladimir's Seminary Press, Yonkers, NY, 2011), pp. 13–26.

[2] For further details with regard to all these see Niederwimmer, *The Didache*, pp. 14, 30–5; Huub van de Sandt and David Flusser, *The Didache: Its Jewish Sources and its Place in Early Judaism and Christianity* (Van Gorcum, Assen/Fortress, Minneapolis, 2002), pp. 59–70; Stewart-Sykes, *On the Two Ways*, pp. 44–146 (with English translations of the texts).

on a first Christian version of the *Two Ways* tractate; a second recension of it formed the basis for yet another version on which the material in both the *Didache* and the *Doctrina apostolorum* were based; and a later recension became the basis for that in the *Apostolic Church Order* and in its *Epitome*. The versions in the remaining texts he judged to be later migrations from the second Christian recension.[3] Alistair Stewart-Sykes has endorsed his conclusions in broad terms, but suggested modifications that we will consider later.

What is particularly interesting about their analysis is that it means that in the relatively short period of Christianity's existence prior to the *Didache* reaching its final state, which is thought to have been around the end of the first century according to many scholars or even earlier according to some, there had already been at least two Christian recensions of the *Two Ways* tractate, and in the following centuries further versions of it were incorporated into these various works, often amplified by the inclusion of other material. Moreover, several scholars have proposed that the addition of the rest of the material in the *Didache* to the *Two Ways* tractate was not all done at one time but involved more than one stage of redaction, either by the same hand or by several editors. While Niederwimmer rejected these various theories, he did acknowledge that the compiler had brought together material from what were already older sources to create the final work. These were: a (written or oral) archaic liturgical tradition concerning baptism and eucharist; a (probably written) also archaic tradition concerning the reception of itinerant charismatics; and a brief apocalyptic description of the events of the end time. This material the compiler expanded and interpreted.[4]

It is no wonder, therefore, that Stanislas Giet described the *Didache* as constituting 'living literature'.[5] This is a genre of material that circulates within a community and forms a part of its heritage and tradition but is

---

[3] Niederwimmer, *The Didache*, pp. 35–41.
[4] *Ibid.*, pp. 42–6.
[5] Stanislaus Giet, *L'Enigme de la Didache* (Ophrus, Paris, 1970), p. 257.

constantly subject to revision and rewriting to reflect changing historical and cultural circumstances. Examples would include folk tales and even some scriptural material, all characterized by the existence of multiple recensions, sometimes exhibiting quantitative differences (i.e., longer and shorter versions) and sometimes qualitative differences (i.e., various ways of saying the same thing, often with no clear reflection of a single *Urtext*), and sometimes both.[6]

What has become increasingly evident in recent years is that not merely do the *Didache* and its related literary works belong to this category but also so does the whole of the church order literature, as scholars gradually abandon the idea that these texts had a single author or editor at a fixed point in time and view them instead as made up of various layers, added and revised over a considerable period of time by various hands as they were transmitted and translated.

The *Apostolic Church Order*

Unlike some of the other church orders, it was long accepted that behind this particular composition lay a redactional history. Thus, Adolf Harnack believed that the compiler had drawn upon five earlier sources: the *Epistle of Barnabas*, an abridgement of the *Didache*, a list of apostles, and two 'pre-catholic compositions of canonical law'.[7] J. V. Bartlet thought that the original had been composed early in the third century, with a first revision at the end of that century and a second in the fourth century.[8] More recently, Bernadette Lemoine also suggested that the work was built up in three successive stages, the first being in the

---

[6] See further Paul F. Bradshaw, 'Liturgy and "Living Literature"' in Paul Bradshaw and Bryan Spinks (eds), *Liturgy in Dialogue: Essays in Memory of Ronald Jasper* (SPCK, London, 1994), pp. 138–53 = (Liturgical Press, Collegeville, 1995), pp. 139–54.
[7] Adolf Harnack, *Die Quellen der sogenannten Apostolischen Kirchenordnung*, TU 2/5 (Hinrichs, Leipzig, 1886), p. 1.
[8] J. Vernon Bartlet, *Church-Life and Church Order during the First Four Centuries* (Blackwell, Oxford, 1943), pp. 99–105.

second century, and the other two in the third century.[9] Stewart-Sykes rejected her conclusions as too simplistic and set out a detailed argument for a more complex process of development. He first made a close examination of the textual variations between the *Two Ways* material in the church order and in its *Epitome* and determined that neither was the source of the other but that both derived from an intermediate version of that material, now lost, a conclusion he shared with Niederwimmer although differing from him with regard to some of the steps in its earlier transmission. The following table illustrating that understanding of the process is adapted from his modification of Niederwimmer's *stemma*.

Figure 3: The relationship of the Two Ways material

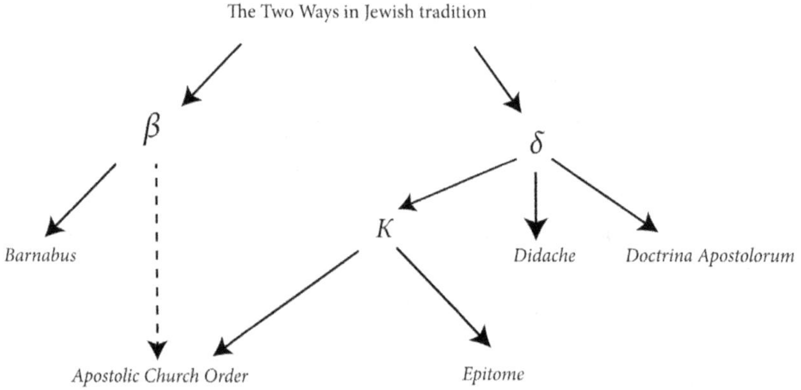

The Two Ways in Jewish tradition

β   δ

K

Barnabus   Didache   Doctrina Apostolorum

Apostolic Church Order   Epitome

The Greek letters *beta* (β) and *delta* (δ) represent two presumed early Christianized versions of the Jewish *Two Ways* material that ultimately led to their incorporation in Barnabas and the *Didache* respectively. The δ strand was also the source of the Latin *Doctrina Apostolorum* and of the supposed

---

[9] Bernadette Lemoine, 'Étude de la notice sur l'évêque dans la Constitution ecclésiastique des apôtres (C.E.A.)' in *Questions liturgiques* 80 (1999), pp. 5–23, esp. p. 12.

intermediate form of the material in the *Apostolic Church Order* and its *Epitome*, a document which Stewart-Sykes designated by the Greek letter *kappa* (κ). This form set the material within the context of a meeting of the apostles and allocated parts of it to each of the eleven in turn (increased to twelve in the final *Apostolic Church Order*), deriving the particular names from an ancient list of the apostles also known to the author of the *Epistula apostolorum* as the two share certain peculiarities.[10] In addition, he believed that the later compiler of the *Apostolic Church Order* itself also had access to the version of the *Two Ways* material in the β strand or at least 'functioned in the same area of tradition', as both of them add a similar eschatological conclusion to the material, which is lacking in both the *Didache* and the *Epitome* and so cannot have been part of that version of the tradition.[11]

In a parallel manner to the editor of the *Didache*, the compiler of the *Apostolic Church Order* not only made minor changes to κ but combined this *Two Ways* tractate with a church order proper that dealt with the ordering of the community's life. Stewart-Sykes rejected Harnack's theory that this half of the work was composed of two distinct sources and argued instead for the use of a single primary source which had been heavily interpolated by the compiler. He judged that all the sources employed in the completed work were of the second century and were either Syrian or Asian in origin. Thus, there was no reason to date the final redaction any later than the early third century, and to regard its provenance as being anywhere other than that of its sources, in contrast to the earlier scholarly consensus that had placed it a century later and in Egypt.[12]

---

[10] On the *Epistula apostolorum*, see Alistair Stewart-Sykes, 'The Asian origin of the Epistula apostolorum and of the new prophecy' in *Vigiliae christianae* 51 (1997), pp. 416–38; C. E. Hill, 'The *Epistula apostolorum*: an Asian tract from the time of Polycarp' in *JECS* 7 (1999), pp. 1–53.

[11] Stewart-Sykes, *The Apostolic Church Order*, pp. 2–33; idem, *On the Two Ways*, pp. 44–9, 53–61, 85–103.

[12] Stewart-Sykes, *The Apostolic Church Order*, pp. 75–9.

The *Didascalia apostolorum*

Until very recently this church order was understood to have been the work of a single individual, composed in the early third century. Although some scholars suspected that small parts of it had undergone a secondary redaction or might be additions to the text, the general consensus was well expressed by R. H. Connolly: 'It would be difficult to find an ancient document in which the marks of a single authorship are more pronounced.'[13] The main exception to this was Chapter 21, concerning the paschal season, where a series of scholars, from Eduard Schwartz in 1905 onwards,[14] believed that they could discern the existence of various levels of material in the text that suggested to them the activity of redactors. One of the most recent to have subjected the chapter to this analysis was Gerard Rouwhorst. He understood there to be three levels within it: an ancient Quartodeciman source; a later hand modifying the prescriptions in an anti-Quartodeciman direction, and a third redactor who supplied apostolic precepts and examples in order to strengthen the instructions.[15]

The view that the work in general constituted a unity was not to deny, however, that there were signs in the text that the compiler had drawn on older sources. In particular, several scholars drew attention to echoes in some places of material in the *Didache*, and both Connolly and Bartlet also recognized the similarity of a passage concerning the appointment of a bishop (2.1.3) to one in the *Apostolic Church Order* (16), but because they believed the latter to be a fourth-century composition, they concluded that it had borrowed from the *Didascalia*

---

[13] R. H. Connolly, *Didascalia Apostolorum* (Clarendon Press, Oxford, 1929), p. xxxvi.
[14] Eduard Schwartz, *Christliche und jüdische Ostertafeln* (Weidmann, Berlin, 1905), pp. 105-21
[15] Gerard Rouwhorst, *Les hymnes pascales d'Ephrem de Nisibe: analyse théologique et recherche sur l'évolution de la fête pascale chrétienne à Nisibe et à Edesse et dans quelques églises voisines au quatrième siècle*, Supplements to *Vigiliae Christianae* 7 (Brill, Leiden, 1989) I, pp. 164-83. See also idem, 'Liturgy on the Authority of the Apostles' in Anthony Hilhorst (ed.), *The Apostolic Age in Patristic Thought* (Brill, Leiden, 2004), pp. 63-85, here at pp. 77-9.

rather than the other way around.[16] The traditional consensus has now been radically challenged by Alistair Stewart-Sykes. Rather than it being a composition by a single hand, he argued that it was made up primarily of a combination of two sources with heavy interpolation and expansion by later redactors. The first of these sources appears to have been a catechetical manual that incorporated some *Two Ways* material, which largely accounts for the echoes of the *Didache*, which are nearly all from the *Two Ways* part of that work. The parallel with part of the *Apostolic Church Order* mentioned above he believed pointed to the second source used in its composition – a derivative of the same church order material that had been used as the second source for that work too.[17]

In other words, while the *Didache* had been composed by appending church-order material to a *Two Ways* tractate, the *Apostolic Church Order* had been composed by combining a similar *Two Ways* tractate with an existing brief church order and the *Didascalia* had used a catechetical manual containing *Two Ways* material together with a derivative of the same church order to form its basis. It seems highly improbable, however, that all three independently decided to adopt the same composite structure for their works as there is no inherent connection between the two types of literature that are used, but they serve quite different purposes. It surely cannot simply be coincidental then, and the compilers of the latter two works must have had some awareness of the *Didache* itself even if they did not use it directly as a source, perhaps because its contents did not fit their needs. Indeed, Stewart-Sykes admitted the possibility of the existence of a direct connection between a redactor of the *Didascalia* 'or of one of its sources' and the *Didache* in order to account for some of the parallels that are not in its *Two Ways* section.[18]

---

[16] Connolly, *Didascalia Apostolorum*, p. 31; Bartlet, *Church-Life and Church Order during the First Four Centuries*, p. 102.
[17] Stewart-Sykes, *The Didascalia Apostolorum*, pp. 11–22.
[18] Ibid., p. 16.

Besides identifying these sources within the *Didascalia*, Stewart-Sykes also claimed to detect three distinct editorial stages that the material had subsequently undergone. In addition to an editor who brought the sources together and worked them over, thus giving the whole composition the impression of a unity, whom Stewart-Sykes therefore terms the 'uniting redactor', he also saw the hand of another later 'deuterotic redactor', who added the last chapter on the freedom of Christians from what is designated as *deuterosis*, the secondary legislation of the Old Testament, as well as several other interpolated passages in the work. The third and final editor he called the 'apostolic redactor', because he appears to have worked over the text to introduce the illusion of explicit apostolic authorship. Chapter 21 he thought had originated in a short Quartodeciman source that the uniting redactor had inserted and modified in order to remove its Quartodeciman chronology, and this too had been edited again by the apostolic redactor.[19] Although he presented arguments in support of this theory, the evidence is not so conclusive as to prove beyond question that there were precisely three principal levels of redaction or that they took place in exactly that sequence, but it is certainly enough to demonstrate that this church order was subject to much editorial activity over a period of time and was not, as previously thought, the work of a single compiler.[20]

In addition to the two major sources, Stewart-Sykes suspected the existence of other smaller sources, like the Quartodeciman one, and of other editorial hands. Although admitting that all these could not be easily identified, he did offer four examples from the text that seemed to point in this direction: in Chapter 12 the directions about seating for worship are interrupted by a direction about prayer; in Chapter 9 a direction about inviting widows to supper appears to belong to a distinct source, as

---

[19] *Ibid.*, pp. 22–44.
[20] But see the qualified support given to his theory by Bart D. Ehrman, *Forgery and Counterforgery: The Use of Literary Deceit in Early Christian Polemics* (Oxford University Press, Oxford/New York, 2013), pp. 344–50.

does material in Chapter 13; and Chapter 18 has parallels in the Pseudo-Athanasian *Syntagma doctrinae* and the related *Fides patrum*.[21] Although he thought that their incorporation had taken place prior to the work of the uniting redactor, it seems quite possible that some of them could be later. Elsewhere, he noted signs that the mention of presbyters, readers, subdeacons, and female deacons were all additions to the core text.[22] The whole process, from the composition of the primary stratum to the final redaction, he judged to have stretched from first century through to the early fourth century. As to provenance, he saw no reason to question the traditional designation of Syria.[23]

The so-called *Apostolic Tradition*

Throughout most of the twentieth century the overwhelming majority of scholars supported the view that this anonymous church order originated in Rome and was the genuine work of Hippolytus, written in the early third century. Even so, a few of them did raise suspicions that what existed in the extant manuscripts was not always what the original author had written.[24] In a series of articles in the latter years of the century, however, Marcel Metzger went much further, developing an idea earlier advanced both by Jean Magne and by Alexandre Faivre, that not only was it not the *Apostolic Tradition of Hippolytus*, it was not the work of any single author at all but rather a piece of 'living literature'.[25] Metzger argued that its lack of unity or logical progression, its frequent

---

[21] Stewart-Sykes, *The Didascalia Apostolorum*, pp. 44–9. See also idem, *On the Two Ways*, pp. 124–46.
[22] Stewart-Sykes, *The Didascalia Apostolorum*, pp. 60–4. See also Paul F. Bradshaw, 'Women and Baptism in the Didascalia Apostolorum' in *JECS* 20 (2012), pp. 641–5.
[23] Stewart-Sykes, *The Didascalia Apostolorum*, pp. 49–55.
[24] See in particular E. C. Ratcliff, 'The Sanctus and the Pattern of the Early Anaphora' in *Journal of Ecclesiastical History* 1 (1950), pp. 29–36, 125–34; A. F. Walls, 'The Latin Version of Hippolytus' Apostolic Tradition' in *Studia Patristica* 3 (1961), pp. 155–62.
[25] Jean Magne, 'La prétendue Tradition apostolique de Hippolyte de Rome s'appelait-elle *Ai diataxeis tōn hagiōn apostolōn*, "Les statuts des saints Apôtres"?' in *Ostkirchliche Studien* 14 (1965), pp. 35–67; idem, *Tradition apostolique sur les charismes et Diataxeis des saints Apôtres* (Paris, 1975), pp. 76–7; Faivre, 'La documentation canonico-liturgique de l'Eglise ancienne', p. 286.

incoherences, doublets, and contradictions, all pointed away from the existence of a single editorial hand. Instead, it had all the characteristics of a composite work, a collection of community rules from quite disparate traditions.[26] Christoph Markschies subsequently added to the doubts about its traditional attribution by pointing out not only that the sole evidence for a connection with Hippolytus was in two of the derived church orders – the title of the *Canons of Hippolytus* and the reference to him in the second subheading of the *Epitome of Apostolic Constitutions* 8 – and these were not added to those works until the late fourth or early fifth century (and thus much too late to credit them with any historical reliability), but also that the mention of 'apostolic tradition' in the prologue and conclusion of the document had been misinterpreted by other scholars and could not allude to the title of the work.[27]

In any case, the tendency to associate documents with apostolic figures or with those believed to have close connections to such persons so as to enhance their authority is very common in the ancient Christian world, and there are certainly other works that are known to have been falsely attributed to Hippolytus.[28] Even the very existence of a document entitled *Apostolic Tradition* by Hippolytus of Rome is not above suspicion. The title is found among an anonymous list of works on the right-hand side of the base of a statue of a seated male figure discovered in Rome in 1551, and as some of these were known works attributed to Hippolytus, the rest were assumed to be also. But this list does not correlate exactly with the works of Hippolytus that are catalogued both by Eusebius and by

---

[26] Marcel Metzger, 'Nouvelles perspectives pour la prétendue Tradition apostolique' in *EO* 5 (1988), pp. 241–59; 'Enquêtes autour de la prétendue Tradition apostolique' in *EO* 9 (1992), pp. 7–36; 'A propos des règlements ècclesiastiques et de la prétendue Tradition apostolique' in *RevSR* 66 (1992), pp. 249–61.
[27] Markschies, 'Wer schrieb die sogenannte *Traditio Apostolica*?'.
[28] See Pierre Nautin (ed.), *Homélies pascales I*, SC 27 (Cerf, Paris, 1950), pp. 34–6; Hanssens, *La liturgie d'Hippolyte*, pp. 84–5; Allen Brent, *Hippolytus and the Roman Church in the Third Century: Communities in Tension before the Emergence of a Monarch–Bishop*, Supplements to *Vigiliae Christianae* 31 (Brill, Leiden, 1995), pp. 192–3.

Jerome. Very surprisingly, it omits those that are most strongly attested as genuinely his, including the commentary on Daniel,[29] and this has led some scholars to propose the existence of two authors or even a school of authors as responsible for the works on the list.[30] In 2002, John Cerrato made an important contribution to the debate by arguing that because Hippolytus was a common name in the ancient world, the various works may be the creations of quite different and unrelated authors from diverse places and that at least some of the works attributed to Hippolytus belonged to an Eastern figure of that name rather than a Roman one.[31] In a final bizarre twist to the tale, archaeological research has revealed that the statue itself was in origin not a representation of Hippolytus at all but of a female figure, which was restored in the sixteenth century as a male bishop because of the list of works inscribed on its base, using parts taken from other statues.[32]

In our commentary on the work, Maxwell Johnson, Edward Phillips and I developed Metzger's conclusions.[33] We agreed that it did not represent the actual practice of any single Christian community but was an aggregation of material from different sources. We judged that this

---

[29] Hanssens, *La liturgie d'Hippolyte*, pp. 229–30, 247–9, 254–82; Brent, *Hippolytus and the Roman Church in the Third Century*, pp. 115–203.

[30] See Pierre Nautin, *Hippolyte et Josipe* (Cerf, Paris, 1947) and idem, 'Notes sur le catalogue des oeuvres d'Hippolyte' in *Recherches de science religieuse* 34 (1947), pp. 99–107; Vincenzo Loi, 'L'identità letteraria di Ippolito di Roma' in *Ricerche su Ippolito*, Studia Ephemeridis Augustinianum 13 (Institutum patristicum Augustinianum, Rome, 1977), pp. 67–88; M. Simonetti, 'A modo di conclusione: Una ipotesi di lavoro' in ibid., 151–6; Paul Bouhot, 'L'auteur romain des Philosophumena et l'écrivain Hippolyte' in *EO* 13 (1996), pp. 137–64.

[31] J. A. Cerrato, *Hippolytus between East and West: the Commentaries and the Provenance of the Corpus* (Oxford University Press, Oxford/New York, 2002).

[32] See Margherita Guarducci, 'La statua di "Sant'Ippolito"' in *Ricerche su Ippolito*, pp. 17–30; eadem, '*La "Statua di Sant'Ippolito" e la sua provenienza*' in *Nuove ricerche su Ippolito*, Studia Ephemeridis Augustinianum 30 (Institutum patristicum Augustinianum, Rome, 1989), pp. 61–74; Hanssens, *La liturgie d'Hippolyte*, pp. 217–31; Brent, *Hippolytus and the Roman Church in the Third Century*, pp. 3–114; and Markus Vinzent, ' "Philobiblie" im frühen Christentum' in *Das Altertum* 45 (1999), pp. 116–17, who made the intriguing proposal that the figure was originally of an Amazon woman named Hippolyta.

[33] Bradshaw, Johnson and Phillips, *The Apostolic Tradition: A Commentary*.

composite character extended to the individual ritual units within the text, such as ordination and baptism, which appeared to be artificial literary creations, made up of layers from different local traditions and from different time periods rather than comprising a single authentic rite that was ever celebrated in that particular form anywhere in the world. Thus, while some of the contents of this church order were more congruent with the second century, other parts had parallels only from the middle of the fourth century. The material also seemed to stem from different geographical regions. Thus, because of its triple interrogation in conjunction with the immersion in water, the core of the baptismal material appears decidedly North African or possibly Roman and the earliest layers of the rest would not have been incompatible with that provenance, but the eucharistic prayer is West Syrian in character, and the later additions to the baptismal material were similarly of an Eastern kind.[34] It is important to note, however, that, just because something is regarded as a later addition to the text, that does not necessarily mean that it is a later composition. In many cases, this may be so, but in others the material may be as old as the core itself, but only added to it at a later date.

Although it is difficult to be precise about where the core material begins and ends, and the extent to which it has been redacted by later hands, it appears that it was formed of three parts, or alternatively three small collections of material were combined to form the initial document:

- directives about appointments to various ministries, to which ordination prayers and other related material were added later,

---

[34] On the West Syrian character of the eucharistic prayer, see Matthieu Smyth, 'The Anaphora of the So-called "Apostolic Tradition" and the Roman Eucharistic Prayer' in Maxwell E. Johnson (ed.), *Issues in Eucharistic Praying in East and West* (Liturgical Press, Collegeville, 2011), pp. 71–97. It should be noted that 'West Syrian' here describes the form of the prayer and not necessarily its precise geographical origin, which could possibly have been Egypt: see Bryan D. Spinks, 'Revisiting Egyptian Anaphoral Development' in David A. Pitt, Stefanos Alexopoulos and Christian McConnell (eds), *A Living Tradition: On the Intersection of Liturgical History and Pastoral Practice; Essays in Honor of Maxwell E. Johnson* (Liturgical Press, Collegeville, 2012), pp. 195–210, here at p. 209.

perhaps at different times, and then a eucharistic prayer and prayers for oil, cheese and olives were interpolated;
- directives about the initiation of new converts without any indication of roles assigned to specific ministers, to which were added later explicit statements about the actions of the bishop and then later still a third layer of more detailed ritual instructions that referred to presbyters and deacons;
- directives about community meals and prayer practices, which were subsequently greatly expanded by several hands.[35]

In some cases, the additions seem to have been drawing on pre-existent written texts, in others they appear as short interpolations amplifying, clarifying or correcting the core material. These many emendations to the core do not readily fall into groups of shared concerns that might have suggested a small number of particular hands at work, but rather point to an extended process of piecemeal revision and updating of the contents. Nor are there any obvious signs of a major editorial figure who conferred a sense unity and purpose to the whole. Indeed, it is continuing presence of grammatical inconsistencies, contradictions, doublets, and incoherent passages that are the major indicators of the composite character of the work.

This approach has won the support of a growing number of scholars, who now refer to the work as 'the so-called *Apostolic Tradition*'. Even Stewart-Sykes, who holds on to a more conservative position, has acknowledged that it 'is not a seamless whole, but appears to be the product of much redactional activity', but he accounts for this by building on the theory put forward by Allen Brent that there was an Hippolytean school of writers at Rome.[36] He posits the existence of three layers within the text: first what he describes as 'an ancient document', and then the

---

[35] For a detailed list of the chapters assigned to the core, see Bradshaw, Johnson and Phillips, *The Apostolic Tradition: A Commentary*, p. 15.
[36] Brent, *Hippolytus and the Roman Church in the Third Century*.

work of two successive redactors, both belonging to this Hippolytean school, one in the late second century and the other (Hippolytus himself) in the middle of the third. The first of these, he believed, was concerned to protect the role of the bishop against powerful presbyters in his community; the second was a presbyter who recognized a single bishop in Rome and saw himself in communion with other presbyters.[37] We, however, would reject the association of much of the document with Rome, and hence with Hippolytus, as there are insufficient parallels with what is known of early Roman liturgy, and would in any case regard the time span as too narrow to account for the advanced nature of some of the liturgical elements in the text.[38] Thus, while it will for convenience continue to be referred to here as the *Apostolic Tradition*, that does not mean that such was its original title.

And on it goes

The character of these church orders as living literature did not end with the composition of the final form of the Greek text. Three of them – the *Didascalia*, the *Didache*, and the *Apostolic Tradition* – were further revised and combined with other material to form the *Apostolic Constitutions*. And the *Apostolic Tradition* itself underwent redaction by two different hands that resulted in the creation of the *Canons of Hippolytus* and of the *Testamentum Domini*. But it was the subsequent copying of all these into later manuscripts, and above all their translation into other ancient languages, that created the context for yet further redaction, sometimes merely with minor changes and small insertions into the text, in other cases with such extensive re-wording and interpolation that they might

---

[37] Stewart-Sykes, *Hippolytus: On the Apostolic Tradition*, pp. 22–32.
[38] See further the debate between Stewart-Sykes and me in *St Vladimir's Theological Quarterly* 48 (2004), pp. 195–206, 233–48, together with a useful summary of the current state of the question by J. A. Cerrato, 'The Association of the Name Hippolytus with a Church Order, now known as *The Apostolic Tradition*' in *ibid.*, pp. 179–94, and a further contribution by Allen Brent, 'St Hippolytus, Biblical Exegete, Roman Bishop, and Martyr' in *ibid.*, pp. 207–31.

nearly be termed new versions rather than translations of the original. The following few examples illustrate something of the range of this editorial activity.

The partial Coptic version of the *Didache* represents an intermediate stage of textual development between the extant Greek and its reworking in *Apostolic Constitutions* 7,[39] and in particular includes a prayer over the oil of anointing (or possibly incense[40]) not found in the Greek text. However, as the version in *Apostolic Constitutions* 7 has a similar prayer at the same point, it would seem that this particular variation already existed in the Greek text as it was known to both the Coptic translator and the compiler of the *Apostolic Constitutions*. Indeed, a few have suggested that it is a genuine part of the original Greek of the *Didache* that was then suppressed for one reason or another by the hand behind the one Greek manuscript that is extant. The majority view is that it is an interpolation.[41]

One family of manuscripts of the Syriac version of the *Didascalia* contains a very different version of the text from that in the other families. There is an introduction setting out the apostolic authorship of the work, an insertion of other church-order material drawn from a variety of sources including the *Testamentum Domini* and the *Apostolic Church Order*, and extensive abbreviation of the text towards the end.[42]

It is in the *Apostolic Tradition*, however, that the greatest deviation in the ancient translations can be seen. Because the Greek original is not extant, it is not possible to compare the reliability of the various translations with that, but they differ so much from one another in many parts of the text that at least some of them cannot be faithfully

---

[39] Rordorf and Tuilier, *La doctrine des douze apôtres*, p. 113.
[40] So claimed Stephen Gero, 'The So-called Anointment Prayer in the Coptic Version of the Didache: A Re-evaluation' in *Harvard Theological Review* 70 (1977), pp. 67–84; and Joseph Ysebaert, 'The So-called Coptic Ointment Prayer of Didache 10.8 Once More' in *Vigiliae Christianae* 56 (2002), pp. 1–10.
[41] See Niederwimmer, *The Didache*, pp. 165–7.
[42] See Stewart-Sykes, *The Didascalia apostolorum*, pp. 261–75.

reproducing what had been in the Greek (or they were using Greek texts that already differed from one another). The diverse ways in which the several translations introduce the presence of other bishops into the directions for the ordination of a bishop that in the Greek had apparently intended that presbyters should conduct the whole proceedings provide an interesting example of this.[43] Within the work as a whole, differences include variations in the order of the material and the omission of several chapters from the Sahidic and Arabic versions (including the texts of the eucharistic and ordination prayers) but not from the Ethiopic translation, which must therefore have been made from a different version of the Arabic than is now extant. On the other hand, the Ethiopic contains longer forms of some of the chapters than exist in the other witnesses, a number of which are very obvious interpolations, the most substantial being an independent set of baptismal prayers. Most remarkable of all has been the recent publication by Alessandro Bausi of a significantly different version of the Ethiopic text that increases our awareness of just how many diverse strands of textual tradition there were to this particular piece of living literature.[44]

---

[43] See Bradshaw, Johnson and Phillips, *The Apostolic Tradition: A Commentary*, pp. 24–7.
[44] See above, p. 17, n. 15.

3

Layers of Tradition

Having recognized the spurious nature of the claim to apostolic authorship made by the church orders, for most of the twentieth century scholars showed a common tendency to view the orders as having been the official regulations of specific Christian communities, their manuals of church law, as it were.[1] Consequently, they were thought to provide a comprehensive and reliable account of the institutions and practices of those communities. So, for instance, Gregory Dix could say of what he believed to be the work of Hippolytus that 'we may safely take it that in outline and essentials the rites and customs to which the *Apostolic Tradition* bears witness were those practised in the Roman Church in his own day, and in his own youth, *c.* A.D. 180'.[2]

However, as time went by, doubts began to be expressed by some as to the status of these documents and so how far they could be taken as descriptive of the normal practices of the churches from which they apparently originated, and how far they were merely prescriptive of practices that might never have actually been put into effect. In particular, Georg Schöllgen argued that their content was not comprehensive but selective: they were polemical texts addressing only specific controverted issues and new situations that had arisen within their communities.[3] Thus, the fact that some institution or practice was not mentioned did not mean that it might not have existed.

---

[1] For an early example, see Maclean, *The Ancient Church Orders*, p. 1.
[2] Gregory Dix, *The Treatise on the Apostolic Tradition of St Hippolytus* (SPCK, London, 1937; 2nd edn 1968 with preface and corrections by Henry Chadwick = Alban Press, London/ Morehouse, Ridgefield, CT, 1992), pp. xxxix–xl.
[3] See Niederwimmer, *The Didache*, pp. 165–7.

Not all were won over to his point of view. Although Niederwimmer gave cautious support with regard to the *Didache*,[4] Bruno Steimer directly challenged Schöllgen, insisting that the church orders represented actual practice and so could be taken as constituting comprehensive mirrors of church life of their times. The absence of actual pseudepigraphy in the *Didache* meant for him that the practices were already generally accepted and had been put into writing by someone recognized as authoritative in the community, while the claims to apostolicity in other works were simply intended to gain them more universal validity.[5]

Steimer's view was in turn subjected to severe criticism by Schöllgen in a review of his book. He argued that the very use of apostolic pseudonymity in the church orders to bolster the authority of what they prescribed counted decisively against the supposition of unanimous acceptance on the part of the intended recipients and against the idea that their authors were authorized representatives of the community. Such a subterfuge would not have been necessary if the authority of what was being prescribed in them had been readily recognized by all concerned.[6] They therefore could not be taken as descriptions of what was already being practised but only as aspirations by their compilers and editors as to what should be practised.

Schöllgen's line of reasoning has been strongly endorsed in a recent major work by Bart Ehrman, who avers that 'when considering the church orders, we are dealing with inherently polemical literature, even when the polemics are below the surface'.[7] Yet, when discussing the *Didascalia*,

---

[4] Niederwimmer, *The Didache*, p. 3, n. 15.
[5] Steimer, *Vertex Traditionis*, pp. 268–80.
[6] Georg Schöllgen, 'Der Abfassungszweck der frühchristlichen Kirchenordnungen: Anmerkungen zu den Thesen Bruno Steimers' in *Jahrbuch für Antike und Christentum* 40 (1997), pp. 55–77. See also idem, 'Pseudapostolizität und Schriftgebrauch in den ersten Kirchenordnungen. Anmerkungen zur Begründung des frühen Kirchenrechts' in Georg Schöllgen and Clemens Schöllgen (eds), *Stimuli: Exegese und ihre Hermeneutik in Antike und Christentum*, Jahrbuch für Antike und Christentum Ergänzungsband 23 (Aschendorff, Münster, 1996), pp. 96–121.
[7] Ehrman, *Forgery and Counterforgery*, p. 387.

he is forced to admit that most of it 'is not polemical in nature' and that the polemic only begins to appear in it when the status of the Jewish Law is raised,[8] although he later rightly adds the discussions of the roles of the bishop and of women as also being controverted issues in the work, following the arguments of Carolyn Osiek and Charlotte Methuen, as well as the form of the observance of Easter.[9]

Rather than viewing the character of the church orders as being strictly polemical, Alistair Stewart-Sykes preferred the more moderate term 'propagandist' to identify their purpose. The principal aim of the redactors of the *Didascalia* he thought was 'to deal with the challenges posed by Jewish Christians';[10] and that of the *Apostolic Church Order* was 'fundamentally to legislate against a liturgical role for women'.[11] The aim of the first of what he believed were the two successive redactors of the *Apostolic Tradition* was 'to boost his particular agendum of exalting the bishop, as a teacher who might be without social standing, above the presbyters, who might act as patrons within the school', while the second, 'as a result of the reconciliation of this school with the wider Roman church,…made it usable in the united community'.[12] For the *Apostolic Constitutions* he referred to the work of Joseph Mueller, who proposed that it reflected an anti-imperial and anti-Nicene stance and that it had adapted traditional techniques of Old Testament exegesis to fit fourth-century ecclesiological contexts.[13] Like Ehrman, however, Stewart-Sykes acknowledged that not every element in the text of these works is

---

[8] *Ibid.*, p. 348.
[9] *Ibid.*, pp. 387–90; Carolyn Osiek, 'The Widow as Altar: The Rise and Fall of a Symbol' in *Second Century* 3 (1983), pp. 159–69; Charlotte Methuen, 'Widows, Bishops and the Struggle for Authority in the *Didascalia Apostolorum*' in *Journal of Ecclesiastical History* 46 (1995), pp. 197–213.
[10] Stewart-Sykes, *The Didascalia Apostolorum*, p. 3.
[11] Stewart-Sykes, *The Apostolic Church Order*, p. 75. On the section concerning the role of women, see further Allie M. Ernst, *Martha from the Margins: The Authority of Martha in Early Christian Tradition*, Supplements to Vigiliae Christianae 98 (Brill, Leiden, 2009), pp. 225–58.
[12] Stewart-Sykes, *On the Apostolic Tradition*, p. 49.
[13] Joseph G. Mueller, *L'Ancien Testament dans l'ecclésiologie des Pères. Une lecture des Constitutions Apostoliques*, Instrumenta Patristica et Mediaevalia 41 (Brepols, Turnhout, 2004), esp. pp. 120–6.

propagandist in intent. Thus, its two sources 'account for the greater part' of the *Didascalia*[14] and similarly the greater part of the *Apostolic Church Order* 'is simply the repetition of traditional material largely derived from earlier documents'[15]; while at the core of the *Apostolic Tradition* was 'an ancient document of a recognized genre'.[16]

No single purpose

However, because of the nature of the church orders as 'living literature', it is not possible to speak of them as having a single identifiable purpose or aim. While the struggle over competing practices and institutions certainly seems to have been the incentive behind the work of some redactors, it is not the sole hermeneutical key to the whole of their contents. Different editorial hands appear to have had quite distinct reasons for doing what they did to the same document. Some emendations merely updated the contents where necessary to reflect what had become by then the norm. A few examples must suffice to illustrate this. As noted in the previous chapter, mention of presbyters, readers, subdeacons and female deacons were all later additions to the core text of the *Didascalia*, which had originally known only the appointment of bishops, deacons and widows.[17] Similarly, the compiler of the *Apostolic Constitutions* converted the injunction in *Didache* 10.7 to 'allow the prophets to give thanks as they wish' into 'allow your presbyters to give thanks' (7.26.6). Furthermore, while the doxological conclusion of the prayer over first fruits in the *Apostolic Tradition* reads simply, 'through your servant Jesus Christ our Lord, through whom be glory to you to the ages of ages. Amen' (31.5), nearly all other conclusions to prayers in the work reveal evidence of clumsy insertions into formulas of this kind to render them more Trinitarian, even at the cost of making them

---

[14] Stewart-Sykes, *The Didascalia apostolorum*, p. 22.
[15] Stewart-Sykes, *The Apostolic Church Order*, p. 80.
[16] Stewart-Sykes, *On the Apostolic Tradition*, p. 49.
[17] See above, p. 35

grammatically incoherent, as in 'through your servant Jesus Christ, though whom to you be glory and power, Father and Son with the Holy Spirit, in the holy church, both now and to the ages of ages. Amen' (7.5).[18] There is no necessary reason to suppose that these and other insertions like them were propagandist or controversial in intent but were simply meant to make the various texts adhere more closely to the orthodoxy and orthopraxis of the particular redactor's era, and which the redactor no doubt supposed must have always been so.

Preserving the imagined past

It will be noticed that in the last example cited above, the new does not entirely replace the old but is instead combined with it to form a hybrid. Although it is not impossible that the editor actually intended the whole of the new composite forms to be used, it seems much more likely that the original has been left undisturbed simply out of a desire to preserve the past, especially as the prayer conclusions thus formed are not ones that were commonly in use in the fourth century as evidenced by contemporary sources. As we shall see, this was not an isolated instance in the church order literature, but points to more complex intentions among redactors, that is, both to update the contents and at the same time as far as possible not to eliminate what had already been there. As the quotations from scholars earlier in this chapter acknowledge, considerable parts of the various church orders have retained traditional material. Its presence often appears to be simply out of respect for what was thought to have been ancient and not because it played any part in controversies of the time. For that reason not everything that was included in the final redaction of a text can necessarily be assumed to represent the current practice of that place and period or even what the redactor desired to be so. A good deal of it may just be the inheritance of the past.

---

[18] See Bradshaw, Johnson and Phillips, *The Apostolic Tradition: A Commentary*, pp. 52–3.

Therefore, the church orders should no longer be read as unified pictures of early church life, whether complete or partial, but as multiple layers of tradition from different times. To begin with a short and relatively simple example, the *Didascalia* includes instructions on how a visiting bishop is to be treated, among which is: 'he should offer the oblation. But if he is sensible and is unwilling, reserving that honour for you, he should speak over the cup'.[19] Marcel Metzger's suggestion that behind this lies the ancient practice of separate short prayers being recited over the eucharistic bread and cup individually, in the manner prescribed in *Didache* 9 and in Jewish custom, which might then be said by different ministers, seems to have won acceptance.[20] This very primitive pattern is unlikely to have continued to be the current practice by the time of the later redaction of this church order – Stewart-Sykes describes the direction as being 'already somewhat archaeological'[21] – but nonetheless it still remained in the text without emendation, quite possibly because its meaning was simply not intelligible to later generations unfamiliar with the custom. It is to be noted that when the *Didascalia* was reworked in the late-fourth-century *Apostolic Constitutions*, in an apparent effort to make some sense of these words, they were converted into an instruction that the visiting bishop should give the blessing to the people (2.58.3).

The compiler of the *Apostolic Constitutions* also did something similar with the directions concerning the baptism of women that came from the *Didascalia*. That earlier text had directed that, at the pre-baptismal anointing of a female candidate, the bishop was to anoint the head alone and that a woman should then anoint the rest of the body so that it would not be exposed to male eyes (3.12). A later hand appears to have added a preference for female deacons rather than women in general to perform

---

[19] *Didascalia* 2.58.3; English translation from Stewart-Sykes, *The Didascalia Apostolorum*, p. 176.
[20] Marcel Metzger, 'The Didascalia and Constitutiones Apostolorum' in *The Eucharist of the Early Christians* (Pueblo, New York, 1978), p. 202.
[21] Stewart-Sykes, *The Didascalia Apostolorum*, p. 78.

the act,[22] with some manuscripts strengthening the prohibition against women other than female deacons touching the oil.[23] The compiler of the *Apostolic Constitutions*, apparently familiar with a different custom in which male deacons rather than the bishop performed the pre-baptismal anointing of the head, then inserted that provision, but still left the reference to the bishop's anointing in its place in the text and merely added at the end a brief instruction that the bishop was to carry out the more recent practice of an anointing after the immersion.[24]

As can be seen (overleaf), the result is confusion, with the bishop seeming to anoint twice, once before the immersion and once after, in addition to the actions of the deacon and deaconess. Sense is restored only when one recognizes that the text as it stands does not accurately represent the current practice known to the compiler, but is an older layer of tradition minimally adapted to incorporate later custom.

These are not the only places where outdated tradition appears to have been retained. In a section of the *Apostolic Tradition* there are instructions relating to common meals. Although in their current state they have been considerably interpolated and display a somewhat confusing air, there is growing agreement that they are part of the most ancient layer of the text and are concerned with the eucharistic meals of quite early Christian communities[25] and that the eucharistic prayer in Chapter 4 is a later addition to this church order, although itself deriving from a quite primitive form that had developed within the West Syrian tradition.[26] The location of this latter prayer, along with prayers over oil,

---

[22] See Bradshaw, 'Women and Baptism in the *Didascalia Apostolorum*'.
[23] Stewart-Sykes, *The Didascalia Apostolorum*, p. 193, nn. 3–4.
[24] English translation of *Didascalia* 3.12 adapted from Stewart-Sykes, *The Didascalia Apostolorum*, p. 193, and of *Apostolic Constitutions* 3.16 made by the author.
[25] Exactly which chapters should be included in this group is not entirely clear. Stewart-Sykes, *On the Apostolic Tradition*, pp. 29–31, regarded Chapters 25–6, and probably also 27, as forming a unit. But it could be argued that part of Chapter 28 along with Chapter 29A and even 30A should also be added: see Bradshaw, Johnson and Phillips, *The Apostolic Tradition: A Commentary*, pp. 146–53, 162–3. Much depends on the particular character ascribed to these meals.
[26] See above. p. 38, n. 34.

Ancient Church Orders

Didascalia 3.12	*Apostolic Constitutions 3.16*
...when women go down into the waters they should be anointed with the oil of anointing by female deacons as they enter the waters. if a woman is present and particularly a female deacon, it is not right that a woman should be seen by a man. But anoint the head alone, with a laying on of a hand. As in ancient times the priests and kings of Israel were anointed, so you should do the same, anointing the head, with a laying on of a hand, of those who come to baptism, both men and women, and subsequently, whether you yourself baptize or command deacons to baptize or presbyters, a woman, a female deacon, as we said above, should anoint the women. But a man should pronounce over them the invocation of the divine names in the water. When she who has been baptized comes out of the waters a female deacon should receive her...	In the baptism of women, the deacon shall anoint only their forehead with the holy oil, and after him the female deacon shall anoint them, for it is not necessary for the women to be seen by men. But only in the laying on of hands shall the bishop anoint her head, as the kings and priests were formerly anointed .... You therefore, bishop, according to that type shall anoint the head of those to be baptized, whether men or women, with the holy oil, for a type of the spiritual baptism. After that, either you, bishop, or a presbyter under you, saying and naming over them the holy invocation of the Father and Son and Holy Spirit, shall baptize them in the water. And let the deacon receive the man, and the female deacon the woman, so that the conferring of the unbreakable seal may take place with dignity. And after that, let the bishop anoint those that are baptized with ointment.

cheese and olives, after the instructions for the ordination of a bishop and prior to those for other ministers looks like an insertion that interrupts the natural sequence, an insertion made by someone who thought that the church order lacked this important element. Either this person or another editorial hand was insistent that the older meal material was 'a blessing and not the eucharist like the body of our Lord' (25=29C), presumably because there was a danger that readers might view it as such, but that does not mean that in much earlier times it had not been thought of as eucharistic, nor does it mean that what was described there was still a living reality in the editor's day as some sort of non-eucharistic agape and not just traditional material retained and given a different interpretation. Even the meal prayers in *Didache* 9–10 might already have been anachronistic by the time of the final redaction of that church order, and it is possible that though the prayers themselves may derive from an older source, the details of the setting in which they were placed in the completed work may be an artificial construct intended to make sense of them and not necessarily reflective of current practice known to the editor.[27]

The radical reworking by the *Canons of Hippolytus* of its principal source, the *Apostolic Tradition*, has been taken as a sign that it was being updated so as to reflect the contemporary experience of the compiler in his native Egypt. Hence his retention of the threefold baptismal interrogation from the original has also been treated as an indication that this too was part of the fourth-century Egyptian rite, even though the church order apparently expected the formula, 'I baptize you in the name…' to be repeated at each of the three immersions, which was rather odd.[28] However, the evidence usually adduced to show that such an interrogation was customary in Egypt at this period is by no means as strong as has previously been thought, and the only place where a baptismal *apotaxis/syntaxis* of a Syrian kind is found in combination with the Romano-African triple interrogation is in the fourth-century Jerusalem liturgy, which is rather a special case.[29] It seems much more likely, therefore, that the *Canons of Hippolytus* presents us here with another instance of the preservation of material from an older source rather than something which had ever been part of the indigenous tradition. The same seems to be true of the parallel retention of the threefold interrogation in the *Testamentum Domini*.[30]

---

[27] See Paul F. Bradshaw, 'Yet Another Explanation of Didache 9–10' in *Studia Liturgica* 36 (2006), pp. 124–8.
[28] See Bradshaw, *The Canons of Hippolytus*, p. 23.
[29] See *Mystagogical Catecheses* 1–2.
[30] See Sperry-White, *The Testamentum Domini*, p. 28.

Literary works rather than practical manuals

What is particularly noticeable about many of the examples quoted above in this chapter is that the attempt to preserve as much of their source as possible often resulted in a lack of clear meaning or simple guidance. On the one hand, this shows how seriously the various editors viewed the material that had come down to them, and strongly implies that they regarded its claim to apostolic authority as genuine and did not wish to abandon its teaching altogether, even when it no longer seemed to have contemporary application. The points at which they felt compelled to add to it or change it were those where it failed to cohere with practices or institutions with which they were familiar or wanted to promote and which they surely thought had equal claim to have originated in apostolic times. Although Bart Ehrman has claimed that those church orders that are actually pseudepigraphical should be viewed as deliberate forgeries because their redactors knew that the attribution was untrue,[31] that judgement is not necessarily accurate. The creation of a fictional apostolic setting for the teaching in the church order or the distribution of its prescriptions to individual apostles can be regarded as merely adding imaginative detail to the basic premise of the apostolic origin of the work that the redactor believed to be true, in a similar way that a dramatized documentary does in modern television productions.

On the other hand, the form that some of their modifications took reveals that the nature of the church orders was changing. The earliest works may well have been intended as manuals of practical instruction to regulate the life of a Christian community. Whoever compiled the *Didache* no doubt wanted its directions to be followed. And the same appears to be true of the *Apostolic Church Order* and at least of the earlier layers of the *Didascalia* and of the *Apostolic Tradition*. When we come to the later recensions of these latter two works, however, the aim appears to be shifting. If we take Chapter 21 of the *Didascalia* as a

---

[31] Ehrman, *Forgery and Counterforgery*, p. 384.

marked example of the process, the intent there certainly seems to be to defend the observance of a Sunday Pascha against a Quartodeciman one by taking an older Quartodeciman source and reinterpreting it. But the practical directions have become submerged in such lengthy, complex and ultimately confusing arguments drawing on biblical authorities that it is apparent that making the case and supporting it with scripture had taken precedence over the instructions themselves. Within the whole of this long chapter, there are really only a few lines of practical directions as such. Although earlier church orders had occasionally undergirded their prescriptions by an appeal to biblical texts, this takes the tendency to a whole new height, which suggests that the editor was much more concerned with engaging in theological debate than with producing a manual suited for practical application.

The later developments within the *Apostolic Tradition* did not employ the same method as those in the *Didascalia*, but they too suggest a declining interest in the practical use of the church order. We have already suggested that the hybrid form of the conclusions of prayers came about for the purpose of promoting doctrinal orthodoxy and not in order to produce a usable liturgical text. The same appears to be true of the various creedal additions that were made to the baptismal material.[32] Furthermore, the composite character of the episcopal ordination rite and the developed horarium of daily prayer including both midnight and cockcrow, whereas fourth-century practice opted for the one or the other, again makes it seem less likely as meant to guide actual practice.

The derivatives of the *Apostolic Tradition* move in quite different directions. While the drastic recasting of the material in the *Canons of Hippolytus* does seem to imply an attempt to render it in a form suitable for actual use (with the possible exception of the retention of the threefold baptismal interrogation), the compiler of the *Testamentum*

---

[32] On the original forms of this, see Maxwell E. Johnson, 'The Problem of Creedal Formulae in *Traditio apostolica* 21.12–18' in *EO* 22 (2005), pp. 159–75.

Domini did not do this in any consistent way, but displayed what was described in Chapter 1 above as 'a perverse fidelity' to his principal source. He retained very many more of the original words and phrases of the *Apostolic Tradition* out of respect for its antiquity, while at the same time interpolating such a large amount of material of his own that neither the sense of the original nor a usable guide to the practices of his own community resulted from it.

Scholars have long debated the purpose of the composition of the *Apostolic Constitutions*, with the aim of propagating particular doctrines being a strong contender. Reviewing such prior suggestions at the end of the nineteenth century, Funk rejected them and claimed that its intention was to rescue ancient documents from oblivion.[33] Much more recently, Metzger adopted a somewhat similar point of view. Describing the work as 'l'apogée de l'ancienne littérature canonique', he identified three traits in it, 'l'importance des traditions recueillies, leur prétention unificatrice et leur revêtement conciliaire'.[34] He was followed by Jardine Grisbrooke: the primary object of its compiler was 'the preservation of existing traditions concerning various ecclesiastical institutions' and 'not to reconcile divergent passages nor to eliminate repetitions, but to retain them if they were part of the traditional material he had inherited'.[35] Of course, 'traditional' here has to include material of a much more recent date that the compiler believed to be ancient.

In any case, it seems impossible to imagine that this church order was ever intended to serve practical ends, even though it incorporates many liturgical elements that seem to be drawn from contemporary Antiochene practice. The effort to rework the material from the *Didascalia* and the *Didache* did not produce what could be a serviceable manual for church life, especially as the resultant eucharistic prayers in Book 7 differ so very markedly from the one in Book 8. Moreover, the

---

[33] Funk, *Die apostolischen Konstitutionen*, pp. 356–61.
[34] Metzger, *Les Constitutions apostoliques* I, pp. 39, 49.
[35] Jardine Grisbrooke, *The Liturgical Portions of the Apostolic Constitutions*, p. 6.

latter is so long and prolix that it is commonly thought that it cannot have been the regular diet of any congregation but was simply intended as a theological essay. Grisbrooke, although questioning the force of the argument from excessive length, thought that the strongest ground for the prayer not having been used much was that its archaic theological expressions would quickly have ruled it out following the decisions of the Council of Constantinople on Trinitarian doctrine in 381.[36]

It is noticeable that these instances of shifts in character that we have identified in the various church orders all seem to belong to the fourth century rather than to the third, and this suggests that it was the changing environment in which the church then found itself that affected the role played by these works. The regulation of ecclesiastical life and its liturgy was becoming less dependent on the remembered past and more subject to the present decisions of bishops, councils and the imperial power. The church orders could no longer function as authoritative practical guides but as treasuries of tradition, albeit tradition that was adapted and supplemented in order to provide literary support for the doctrinal positions and liturgical preferences of its later redactors.

Descriptive or prescriptive?

We return to the questions with which this chapter began. Were the church orders in any sense the 'official' publications of Christian communities, or does their reliance on an alleged apostolic pedigree suggest the opposite? And can we presume that they were comprehensive in their coverage and thus provide a full description of their communities' institutions and practices, or did they deal only with controversial issues and/or were promoting what were only minority views within their particular locality?

Schöllgen's argument that the recourse to apostolic authority is an indicator that the contents of church orders would not have been

---

[36] *Ibid.*, p. 21.

accepted by all of their intended recipients is one that has force, but that does not mean that they are solely composed of controversial material or are exclusively propagandist in intent. As we have seen, fundamental to the whole collection was the desire to preserve what had come down from antiquity out of respect for its apostolic origin, even though that included the addition by redactors of contemporary elements falsely supposed to be ancient that were absent from the written texts that lay before them. Not all of these additions can be presumed to be the subject of controversy. Some certainly appear to have been so and required the support of biblical citations and theological arguments. But others seem to have been added simply because the editors thought that they had always existed and so should be there. Even so, the church orders do not necessarily provide us with a complete and reliable picture of church life at the time of their redaction. Some elements contained in them were already obsolete and retained simply out of reverence for the supposed source, while other aspects of ecclesiastical life may not be mentioned at all if there was not something significant to be said about them.

Above all, just because something was prescribed does not mean that it was actually practised at the time. For instance, it has been suggested that the concept in 1 Corinthians 12–14 of a wide variety of different gifts of the Spirit being exercised by different members of the congregation was not operative outside the churches that came under Pauline influence, and perhaps not even fully operative within them. Just because Paul believed that certain things should be so does not necessarily mean that they were so.[37] How much more likely, then, that the church orders contain (a) elements that had once existed but were no longer current, being retained simply out of respect for their imagined apostolic origin; (b) elements that existed in the present and were generally accepted by Christians of the time, (c) elements that were there with controversial

---

[37] See, for example, Margaret Y. MacDonald, *The Pauline Churches* (Cambridge University Press, Cambridge, 1988), pp. 51–60.

or propagandist intent, endorsed by some communities but opposed by others, and perhaps even (d) elements that were the product of the idiosyncratic beliefs of the editor alone and not actually in existence anywhere.

Influence

At least one further question remains. Did anyone take any notice of the church orders? Although there is insufficient evidence to answer this question definitively, we can take note of the languages into which they were – and were not – translated as constituting markers of the extent and limits of their impact. Although the *Two Ways* material seems to have spread rather widely in the ancient Christian world, the church orders themselves appear to have had more restricted spheres of influence. With the possible exception of the earliest stratum of the *Apostolic Tradition*, all of them seem to have originated somewhere in the East, Syria and Egypt being the most prominent locations. Nor did they subsequently arouse much interest in the West, and that included the *Apostolic Tradition*, the later history of which lies almost entirely in the East. The only Latin translation known is the Verona palimpsest containing the *Didascalia*, the *Apostolic Church Order* and the *Apostolic Tradition*. There may perhaps have been a Latin translation of the *Didache*, but that is by no means certain.

Even later Syrian interest in the church orders seems to have been rather limited. While there may perhaps once have been a Syriac translation of the *Didache*, neither the *Apostolic Tradition* nor the *Canons of Hippolytus* are known to have existed in that language. Conversely, there is no firm evidence that the whole of the *Didascalia* was ever translated into Coptic, nor the first seven books of the *Apostolic Constitutions*.

Thus, it was in Egypt, and ultimately in Ethiopia, that the majority of the church orders seem to have found a home and continued to be translated and copied in later centuries. Moreover, the absence of the Greek original of several of the church orders provides another indicator of the declining interest in these works in other churches as they were allowed to disappear and new copies were not made. Again, the explanation for this development is provided by the ecclesiastical context. Authority in the Chalcedonian churches now rested with Ecumenical councils and patriarchal sees, and so it was primarily in the churches of Egypt and Ethiopia that appeal to alleged apostolic precedent continued to flourish and resulted in the eventual preservation of these fascinating and complex documents, much to the benefit of modern scholars.

From 1987 to 2004, the Joint Editorial Board of the two sponsoring agencies commissioned numbers 1–58 of *Joint Liturgical Studies*, published by Grove Books Ltd (see the Grove Books website or end-pages of previous *Joint Liturgical Studies*). In 2005, SCM-Canterbury Press Ltd, now Hymns Ancient and Modern, became the publishers. Two titles (of 48–64 pages) are published each year. Prices are £5.95 or £6.95 for back-numbers (not all are in print), **£7.95** for nos. 74 and all the numbers thereafter.

59 (2005) *Proclus on Baptism in Constantinople* by Juliette Day
60 (2005) *1927-28 Prayer Book Crisis in the Church of England Part 1: Ritual, Royal Commission, and Reply to the Royal Letters of Business* by Donald Gray.
61 (2006) *Prayer Book Crisis…Part 2: The cul-de-sac of the 'Deposited Book'…until further notice be taken* by Donald Gray.
62 (2006) *Anglican Swahili Prayer Books* by Ian Tarrant.
63 (2007) *A History of the International Anglican Liturgical Consultations 1983–2007* by David Holeton and Colin Buchanan.
64 (2007) *Justin Martyr on Baptism and Eucharist* edited by Colin Buchanan
65 (2008) *Anglican Liturgical Identity: Papers from the Prague meeting of the International Anglican Liturgical Consultation* edited by Christopher Irvine
66 (2008) *The Psalms in Christian Worship: Patristic Precedent and Anglican Practice* by Anthony Gelston
67 (2009) *Infant Communion from the Reformation to the Present Day* by Mark Dalby
68 (2009) *The Hampton Court Conference and the 1604 Book of Common Prayer* edited by Colin Buchanan
69 (2010) *Social Science Methods in Contemporary Liturgical Research: An Introduction* by Trevor Lloyd, James Steven and Phillip Tovey
70 (2010) *Two Early Egyptian Liturgical Papyri: The Deir Balyzeh Papyrus and the Barcelona Papyrus* translated and edited by Alistair Stewart
71 (2011) *Anglican Marriage Rites: A Symposium* edited by Kenneth Stevenson
72 (2011) *Charles Simeon on The Excellency of the Liturgy* by Andrew Atherstone
73 (2012) *Ordo Romanus Primus: Latin Text and Translation with Introduction and Notes* translated and introduced by Alan Griffiths.
74 (2012) *Rites Surrounding Death: The Palermo Statement of the International Anglican Liturgical Consultation 2007* edited with Introduction and Commentary by Trevor Lloyd
75 (2013) *Admission to Communion: The Approaches of the Late Medievals and the Reformers* by Mark Dalby
76 (2013) *Gaudius of Brescia on Baptism and the Eucharist* by Dominic Keech
77 (2014) *Liturgical Language and Translation: The Issues Arising from the Revised English Translation of the Roman Missal* edited by Thomas O'Loughlin
78 (2014) *Further Essays in Early Eastern Initiation: Early Syrian Baptismal Liturgy* by Paul Bradshaw and Juliette Day
79 (2015) *Eighteenth-Century Anglican Confirmation: Renewing the Covenant of Grace* by Phillip Tovey
80 (2015) *Ancient Church Orders* by Paul F. Bradshaw

The Sign refreshed and improved for 2015!

Are you a parish magazine editor looking for good quality well written content to supplement and enhance each issue you produce?

If the answer is yes, then we can help... we are delighted to announce that **The Sign** has been refreshed and improved for 2015 to give you even better articles, ideas, reviews, puzzles and the lectionary for the month - all to add to your local content. A4 and A5 formats are available.

For more information on ordering **The Sign** please call **01603 785910 or email vanessa.butcher@hymnsam.co.uk**

If you're interested in advertising in **The Sign** which reaches a readership of 60,000 each month, **please contact Stephen Dutton on 0207 776 1011 or email stephen@churchtimes.co.uk**
Display and lineage ad space available.

Subscribe for just £3 for the first 3 issues!*

 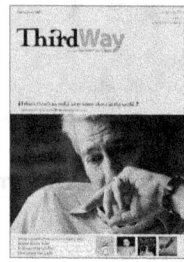  

Every issue of Third Way includes features on social or cultural issues and interviews high-profile people from those fields.

Third Way also reviews films, music, books and television.

Why not contact us today to take advantage of this special introductory offer!

 01603 785910    subs@thirdway.org.uk

CODE: TW15AD

*Then £15 by direct debit every 6 months thereafter

NEW FROM CANTERBURY PRESS

Of Water and the Spirit

Mission and the Baptism Liturgy

As the Church of England alone conducts more than 2500 baptisms each week and the number of adult candidates rises steadily, this robust and original study explores baptism as an expression of the church's mission.

Phillip Tovey explores baptism and confirmation in the Christian tradition through the lens of a biblical theology of baptism.

Beginning with the practices and liturgies of the New Testament church, he traces their development through the early Christian centuries, the Middle Ages, the Reformation and its aftermath, in the context of world mission and in the modern secular age.

978 1 84825 803 7   160pp   Available now   £16.99

www.canterburypress.co.uk

www.ingramcontent.com/pod-product-compliance
Lightning Source LLC
Chambersburg PA
CBHW071321080526
44587CB00018B/3304